The Leader's Edge

The Leader's Edge

Using Personal Branding to Drive Performance and Profit

Susan Hodgkinson

iUniverse, Inc.

New York Lincoln Shanghai

The Leader's Edge
Using Personal Branding to Drive Performance and Profit

iUniverse books may be ordered through booksellers or by contacting:

iUniverse
2021 Pine Lake Road, Suite 100
Lincoln, NE 68512
www.iuniverse.com
1-800-Authors (1-800-288-4677)

Because of the dynamic nature of the Internet, any Web addresses or links contained in this book may have changed since publication and may no longer be valid.

The views expressed in this work are solely those of the author and do not necessarily reflect the views of the publisher, and the publisher hereby disclaims any responsibility for them.

ISBN: 978-0-595-35989-9 (pbk)
ISBN: 978-0-595-67307-0 (cloth)
ISBN: 978-0-595-80440-5 (ebk)

Printed in the United States of America

To my husband Russell, and my children Emily, Matt, and Julia, for their extraordinary commitment, support, and personal generosity.

With lifelong gratitude to Dianne and Gerald Lynch, and to my lifelong friend Taryn Chiarella.

In memory of Doris Richards McGowan and Maureen McGowan Hodgkinson.

Contents

Foreword

I was both honored and delighted when Susan Hodgkinson asked me to write the Foreword for her book on Personal and Leadership Branding. I know first-hand the power of Susan's techniques for making each of us more effective in our "marketplace." She first began working with me as my executive coach seven years ago. She has helped my staff work more effectively as a team. She has trained 1,000 professionals of color in my organization, The Partnership, on how to take responsibility for managing their careers successfully. The brilliance of Susan's Personal and Leadership Branding approach is that it is pragmatic and doable, and it produces powerful results.

I met Susan in 1997 when a colleague recommended her Personal Branding approach for a conference that The Partnership was sponsoring. The room was "abuzz" at the end of her seminar. These professionals were excited and energized to learn that *they* control their success and that there are tools to help them achieve their professional goals. At the conference I was impressed with the clarity and power of Susan's techniques. Fortunately for me, she was impressed with my leadership and the work of The Partnership, a non-profit that assists Boston businesses to more effectively attract, retain, and advance professionals of color. She promptly offered to become my Personal coach.

Prior to Susan's coaching I had been quite successful in building a "brand" for The Partnership. However, I had never considered that I too have a "brand" and that it was important for me to manage it. I knew it was important to the success of The Partnership that our programs be well defined, measurable, and add demonstrated value. It never occurred to me that *my* success also required a clear vision, demonstrated values, and measures of my worth in the marketplace. I knew the future of The Partnership depended upon communicating its quality, integrity, and quantitative impact. Susan's process has given me the confidence and techniques to be equally thoughtful, purposeful, and deliberate about the messages I want to convey about myself. Susan's methods are performance-oriented and results-oriented. They are as effective with a group as they are with individuals. Her techniques for building one's personal brand literally helped to transform The Partnership staff. She led every member through a self-assessment process about their "brand"—their role, value, and contribution to the organization—and how they formally and informally communicated their "persona" within and outside the organization. This rigorous process was instrumental to The Partnership staff shifting from a personality driven culture into a well defined team that is aligned, productive, and focused on outcomes.

The most poignant testament to the power of Susan's methods is the impact she has had on the 1,000 professionals she has trained in The Partnership's retention and development programs. Many people of color are raised to believe if you are good at what you do, the rest will follow. Culturally, self-promotion is viewed as inappropriate behavior. Susan's Personal and Leadership Brand approach has empowered these professionals to appreciate that *they are responsible for managing their careers*. Her exercises illustrate the difference between self-promotion and being conscious about what people know and think about you. Her tools and strategies teach the value of preparing what you want the audience to know about you—prior to every meeting, every speech, and every interaction.

After working with Susan, I recognized that each of us has a "brand" in the environments in which we work and live, i.e., people are constantly forming impressions about us through our own behavior and from what others say about us. It is our responsibility to insure that those impressions are reflective of who we are—our vision, our character, our values, and our contributions. Susan's process gives insights into the formal and informal ways in which we communicate (or don't communicate) our intentions and worth. For example, after reading this foreword you have formed an impression of Susan and her work. When you read and use the strategies in this book, I strongly believe you will discover insights into achieving your career goals, and, in the process, come to appreciate Susan's "brand" as an experienced, savvy, and results-oriented businesswoman.

Benaree P. Wiley
President and CEO, The Partnership

Preface

The most successful people I know manage their careers as closely as they manage all of the other important things in their lives: their marriages, their health, and their money, just to name a few. They conduct routine check-ups on their professional lives, and they perform routine maintenance to keep things running smoothly. Rather than leaving things to chance, they take an active role in charting their career progress to make sure they achieve their short-term and long-term goals. And because they take these steps, they are more likely to get where they want to be. As a result, they usually have interesting and lucrative careers.

They are able to accomplish their goals because they think of themselves and their careers as *brands,* and they are as relentless in managing their brands (how they live in the hearts and minds of those in their markets) as are companies whose brands are household names. This thinking helps them develop, manage, and promote themselves just as companies develop, manage, and promote their successful brands. When you start to think of yourself as a brand, you begin to understand the steps you have to take to manage and grow that brand for it to be successful.

The method I use with my clients to help them understand and define their brands is called the 5 P's of Leadership Brand®, and it is the focus of this book. The 5 P's are persona, product, packaging, promotion, and permission. When understood and managed with great discipline, the 5 P's enable you to create a powerful brand for yourself as a supplier of services where you work. It provides you with the tools and processes needed to be your own brand manager: to identify your unique value, to bring it to market in a way that creates great impact, and to ensure that how you understand yourself is in fact aligned with how others understand you.

I wrote this book for talented, motivated leaders at all levels in organizations to introduce them to an approach to professional development that can engender a realistic, equitable, dynamic, powerful, and sustainable relationship between them and the businesses to which they devote their energies. My methodology, which builds on the proven business principles that great companies have espoused and applied for decades, is unique in that it takes these ideas to the next level—the individual level—where ultimate accountability and greatness reside. I have worked with thousands of professionals throughout the U.S., including senior executives and middle managers, as well as individual contributors, and have helped them apply this model to themselves to achieve greater impact and success at work. It can do the same for you.

Acknowledgments

This book is a composition that is enriched with the voices of many professionals of different levels, experiences, talents, colors, and backgrounds. I am deeply grateful to the many teachers whose invaluable lessons have helped me grow and develop over the course of my life and career, and to those whose belief in this work and shared passion for it have fueled its growth and impact.

I would like to acknowledge the extraordinary energy, passion, creativity, and substance of my cherished friend and colleague, Alesia A.W. Latson, and her contributions to this book. Alesia's insights and exceptional commitment have had as profound an impact on the writing of this book as they have had in my life overall, and for this I am especially grateful.

In leaving corporate life a decade ago to launch my practice, I could not have imagined the level of professional satisfaction and personal fulfillment that I would experience working with the exceptional people whom I am privileged to call my clients. I hold our work together in highest esteem, and honor you for the powerful impact you have through your work around the world.

Introduction

Think about the strongest brands you know. What are they? You perhaps thought of Coca Cola, IBM, Sony, or others. Now, think about people in your organization who have brands just as strong as Coke, IBM, and Sony. Who are the people who come to mind? Did you list your own name in that group? If you didn't, why didn't you?

Having and *owning* a strong brand—a brand so powerful that it towers above other "also rans" in its market—is a choice. It's 100% controllable. It's the reflection of a decision on the part of its owner, and a commitment to use the necessary levels of rigor and discipline to achieve and sustain that market leader status.

The old employment-for-life contract is gone. The forces thriving in today's business marketplace—unprecedented competition, consumer demands for highest quality, fastest response times, and lowest prices, off-shoring in pursuit of cost control—these and so many others are forces the worlds' strongest brands must deal with every day. The owners of strong personal and leadership brands are tackling these same challenges as they continuously build their own strong brands. And how about you? Your key to success is to take charge—to see yourself as a brand in a marketplace and to work continuously to manage your brand successfully. When you do this, you will become known for consistently delivering distinctive quality and value. Providing compelling value ensures that there will always be a satisfying role for you in your organization's future. Using the 5 P's will help you achieve this success.

The 5 P's of Leadership Brand®

The 5 P's of Leadership Brand® are persona, product, packaging, promotion, and permission. These 5 P's may sound familiar. This model is rooted in the classic marketing and brand management practices that the best companies have employed consistently and relentlessly for decades to remain market leaders. Since developing the 5 P's in the mid-1990s, I have refined the methodology based on my experience with several thousand individuals who have used this framework to take charge of their careers. The 5 P's are the foundation of all strong personal and leadership brands.

Persona is the emotional connection and reaction you elicit from other people as a result of your personal energy and style. It's the outward manifestation of your vision, values, attitude, and worldview. It's the visceral reaction others have to you, one human being to another. Knowing how your style affects others, and modulating that style to ensure positive and productive exchanges, is essential to your success.

Product is the sum of your qualifications, experience, technical and/or functional expertise, ideas, and results you've delivered over time.

Packaging is the wrapping you place around your product. It includes your personal appearance and your surroundings, such as your office. It also includes how you package your work—the presentation of your ideas in reports or other written materials.

Promotion concerns how you inform your market about your value and impact (the sum of your persona and product). If you are in a leadership role, it also includes how you will promote the accomplishments of your team.

Permission is your sense of legitimacy, your internal confidence and core belief that you have important contributions to make, and therefore don't need to wait for anyone else to invite you to do so.

The 5 P's represent the elements in a comprehensive brand management system that, when implemented and managed correctly, help you define, develop, and control your value exchange within your organization (your marketplace). In Chapter 1, you will be provided with context for thinking about your own brand. Chapters 2–6 address the 5 P's, and show you how to utilize them to define, develop, and manage your brand. Chapter 7 explains the importance of getting frequent feedback, and shows you how to get it from your marketplace to insure a powerful value exchange.

Throughout the book, you will have many opportunities to think about your own brand in relation to the 5 P's. As you do so, you will be filling in your Brand Development Plan Worksheet (a blank form can be found at the back of the book) to help you define your brand, promote it, and manage it to create success for your organization and more professional choices for yourself.

I've also provided a Suggested Reading list, which gives information on resources mentioned in many of the chapters.

Let's begin by developing an awareness of your current brand.

Chapter 1

Developing an Awareness of Your Leadership Brand

There's a story I like to tell that illustrates the importance of being aware of your brand and the way other people see you. This story will help you understand what a brand is and its importance to your career.

I was playing golf with a client, Mary (names used throughout the book are fictitious), her boss (the CEO), and Larry (a manager who reported to Mary). The CEO, Mary, and I arrived early; Larry was late. The conversation went something like this:

CEO: So, how do you think Larry's doing?

Mary: I think he's doing pretty well. He managed the team out of that major production disaster they had last year, and he's on the rebuild—I think the next couple of quarters will be pretty decent. (Pause) How do *you* think Larry's doing?

CEO: Let me level with you, Mary. I think Larry's a good guy, but I have two concerns. He has a tendency to be unduly upbeat about his business, which makes me wonder about his business judgment—does he really believe his own hype? If so, I think he's got some serious issues with judgment. I also worry that I don't have the full picture of his business, and that I'm going to be surprised, probably unpleasantly. So there's a fundamental trust issue there. The other thing that bothers me about Larry is that the guy is always late. That makes me wonder if he's disorganized or just plain dumb. You need to know I've got some real questions about him.

Mary: I see…oh, here he is now.

Larry (big smile, upbeat voice, hand outstretched): Good morning! Gee, sorry I'm a few minutes late—I got here a while ago and you weren't here so I went to make some calls. (Mary and the CEO exchanged a knowing glance. Larry's comment about making calls, meant to counteract his tardiness, wasn't having the positive effect he had hoped for.)

CEO: So, Larry, how's it been going? How's business?

Larry (with another big smile): Wow—business has never been better. Of course, we took care of that small production glitch we had months back, and we're looking at a really strong set of numbers this year. In fact, if things keep going the way they have been, I think this will be a record year for us. The team's just hitting it out of the park. Yes, it's going really, really well.

By the first sentence of his reply, Larry had lost the CEO. If he had been paying closer attention, he'd have noticed that the CEO was sending subtle but disparaging glances to Mary, Larry's *manager,* as if to say, "See, I told you so. The more he talks, the less I trust him and what he's saying."

Poor Larry. As I listened to this interaction and watched Larry dig his own grave, I realized that he had no idea about his brand according to his CEO. I was pretty sure that he would have behaved differently if he had known.

Conversations like this go on all the time. Perhaps you have had them yourself. Do you think the person who's the subject of the conversation is *aware* of the viewpoints others have? Wouldn't most people change self-sabotaging behavior if they were aware of its cost? Conversely, might some of us be even more successful if we had the self-confidence that comes from knowing how much we and our work are genuinely respected and valued? Larry's tardiness and overly optimistic forecasts cost him a lot that day on the golf course, but I don't think he was remotely aware of it. He didn't know that every word and action reinforced an impression (unfortunately, a negative one) that his CEO had of him.

Why do I think it's important for you to read this story? Because it illustrates how powerful a reputation is—how it serves as a reference point that we constantly reinforce with our words and actions. It illustrates how easy it is to be unaware of the impressions we make. Your actions say things about you, whether you are aware of them or not. As we all know, most impressions and perceptions are very difficult to change.

Impressions and perceptions contribute to what your boss and your co-workers think of you and the way they describe you to others. They become part of how you are perceived—your brand. Everyone has a brand. Your brand is the identity you own in the hearts and minds of your boss, staff, customers, senior management, and colleagues. And it affects *everything* at work: how receptive others are to your ideas, your ability to lead and bring about meaningful changes, your subordinates' careers, the impression your new boss will have of you before you have even met, how much you get paid, whether and when you get promoted or selected to lead important assignments, and whether you are on the winning or losing end of the next reduction in force. That is why it is essential that you take charge of your brand, and then manage it aggressively over the course of your career.

What Is a Leadership Brand?

In the simplest terms, a brand is like a mosaic, made up of many different impressions that combine to form a picture of you in someone else's mind. Ideally, the brand you have in your market is the identity or reputation you have *chosen*. In other words, the way you are perceived, experienced, and appreciated by other people is exactly the way you want to be perceived, experienced, and appreciated. Brand management involves making sure these two—your *intentions* and the *reality* of your brand to others—are always aligned, always in harmony.

Your brand is rooted in your core values. It comes from deep within you, and it is based on your beliefs. It is *not* something you develop because you think it is the way others want you to be. Only you know what your core values are and what you believe in deeply, just as you know best what your differentiated capabilities are and how to deploy them in a way that brings you great fulfillment and affords you major impact where you work. Thus, only you can know what kind of brand you want to have.

Your brand is made up, first, of your intentions and, second, of how your intentions manifest themselves to others. Others hold their sense of you in their minds—they develop a picture of you through the compilations of different impressions they get of you. Where do these impressions come from? For Larry, in the story above, they came from the CEO's direct experience with him. Direct experience is the most powerful way we gather data about people or products or services or businesses. But there are other ways too, including stories we hear, perceptions, beliefs, and biases of those with whom we interact.

Leadership brands are developed and managed in much the same way as are corporate brands. Just as people form impressions of products, they form impressions of you. Your leadership brand is a result of stories people hear about you, as well as direct and indirect experiences they have had with you. Stories play an active role in shaping brands because organizations are inherently social—they run on relationships. What are the stories told about you at work? Who is telling them and why? What is their special interest? Is your manager acting as your *agent* because of how impressed he or she is with your performance? You have considerable influence over the stories told about you and how you are understood at work. In later chapters, you will learn how to make the stories reinforce your desired brand, and what to do if they don't create the impressions you intend to have.

In addition to stories, what other ways do people have indirect exposure to you? Do your written reports get forwarded to others, for example? Who gets them? How often? Does your staff share thoughts, experiences, impressions about you with others?

Beliefs and predispositions also factor into what people think about brands. Our own values dictate what we pay attention to—even how we hear (or don't) and interpret the words of others. If someone introduces you to a new colleague by saying, "I'd like you to meet Bob—he's a real risk-taker," you will interpret this information based on your own beliefs about and experience with risk-taking.

Strong Brands Are Managed Outcomes

You are in charge of your own outcomes, the impact you have on your business, and your future choices and opportunities. You control the quality of your brand because you control the *experience and impact of you*. You determine your own destiny. Isn't that great, and perhaps a little scary?

To fully manage your brand at work, it helps to understand that your brand has two dimensions: your self-definition (your own sense of who you are and the value you bring to your organization and its customers) and the compilation of the perceptions (based on all kinds of data) held about you by others in your organization. Do others' perceptions really matter? Should we really care about what others think? The answer is yes. We need to know what others think in order to find out if their perceptions are aligned with our own. We don't work in a vacuum. Organizations are social systems, after all. If you want to persuade or lead others, you must have internal clarity about who you are as a person and a professional, and about your vision of the future of the business.

The reality is that what others think *does* matter. Suppose you think your willingness to 'take a stand' on tough issues is one of your core strengths. Do you know if others in your organization would agree with your assessment? Would they see your willingness to stand alone as courageous and point to business improvements as outcomes, or would they say you're just being contrary—the 'resident critic'? Would they say you are just criticizing and striking down others' ideas and work without offering alternatives, leaving demoralized colleagues and dead projects in your wake?

How we're experienced and understood matters because it affects our ability to get results. The stronger and more substantive our brand, the more likely we are to be able to innovate, take risk, and drive for break-through results because those around us will support our efforts. Think of Larry at the golf course. Larry reinforced the existing concerns the CEO had about him, digging himself deeper into trouble with every passing conversation. "Overly-optimistic," "can't trust him to give the balanced picture," and "always late" are three dominant aspects of Larry's brand identity in the mind of the person running the company. And Larry did it to himself—the personal experience he created drove the CEO's percep-tion of him. If Larry had done what all great brand managers do, if he had gathered feedback to understand how he is experienced by others, he might have acted differently to reposition himself in the mind of the CEO. This isn't about how to fit in or be more popular; it is about getting results by leveraging your own unique capabilities while operating in a social sys-tem. Thus, managing your brand involves the following:

- Knowing who you are and what's important to you, and connecting passionately to your work.

- Knowing which existing strengths to defend or grow, when to embrace feedback, and when to take steps toward self-improvement so you can be even better at what you do.

- Identifying and celebrating your uniqueness as the center of your brand value exchange. Do you own your own niche of excellence at work? If so, what is it and how do you continuously grow it? If not, why not, and what are the implications of that for you and your business?

Superior Marketing Is Central to Strong Brands

Marketing is all about *creating exchanges of value between a supplier and a buyer*. The American Marketing Association defines marketing as the process of planning and executing the conception, pricing, promotion, and distribution of ideas, goods, and services to *create exchanges* that sat-isfy individual and organizational objectives. Marketing is *not* spin, hype, slogans, bait and switch, over-promising and under-delivering, setting unrealistic expectations to get fleeting publicity, or anything of that sort. Every one of us knows that claims that can't be backed up backfire. This book will challenge you to develop and deliver your own *powerful exchange of value,* for the benefit of your customers, your business, and yourself.

How Strong Is *Your* Brand?

Your Brand's ROI

The best way to manage your leadership brand is to use the framework of the 5 P's as you assess and continuously strengthen your *brand value.* This value is also known as your brand's Return on Investment (ROI). The ultimate measure of a strong leadership brand is its payback in economic terms to the organization and its customers. How much money did you (along with your team and others) make or save for your organization last year? Last month? Sales reps usually have a much easier time answering that question than do other suppliers of service to the organization—for example, those in staff roles. And yet, everyone has a P&L, and everyone can and should know how their work drives bottom line results. For many leaders, answering this question means understanding their impact in the context of a team or teams, and the work that many do to achieve a shared result. The objective is to hold yourself accountable for knowing the economic impact of what you do. Especially for women and people of color, this knowledge, and what you do with it and about it, can have a significant leveling effect on the organization's playing field. If you are a meaningful contributor to revenue growth or expense reduction, or both, and you can describe it in economic terms, and you share it with others who need to know, you place yourself in a position of strength and opportunity at work. If you don't hold yourself accountable for doing this analysis, maximizing it, and communicating it, you allow others to control your destiny.

Doing the Math: How to Calculate Your Own ROI

While the calculations for individual positions and roles include different inputs and considerations, the key to analyzing your ROI is finding a line of sight between your activities and achievements and how they show up as revenue gains or expense reductions in your organization's P&L. As noted, this can be particularly difficult for those in staff functions, but it is still quite achievable and very important. Here is an example for a Human Resources (HR) Team Leader, who heads a team of five HR generalists. In this example, we will take just one aspect of the HR leader's achievements over the past twelve months.

Goal: Reduce annual turnover of designated "A" players from 12% to 8% across lines of business served.

Measure: In raw numbers, on a base of 350 "A" players, reduce the number leaving from 42 to 28 (net save of 14 of the organization's top talent).

Tactics: Improve the coaching skills of those managing these players, starting with at-risk talent. Emphasize career development, build quality development plans, ensure managers and players meet on the plan quarterly, and check in on progress.

- Assign trained senior mentors to each player.
- Hold managers accountable through compensation for the retention effort.
- Improve the managerial skills of weaker managers to support retention targets.

Result: Goal of net save of 14 met.

Economic impact: Using a combination of company research and industry data, the estimated replacement cost per "A" player is 125% of salary and benefits. If the average salary and benefits per player is $150,000, replacement cost is then $150,000 x 125% = $187,500. The total saved through

and can be costly to your organization and to you. People who have strong brands hold themselves accountable for coming up with solutions and taking the necessary action to implement them.

Service suppliers think in terms of the pursuit of excellence. Try this exercise: Using just a few words, write down what you, as a service supplier, are in business to do. What services do you provide? Underneath this list, write what excellence looks like in your line of work. Said another way, what does it mean to be the *very best* at what you do? Take a few minutes and really think about it. Now, reflect on what you have written. Was it difficult to come up with a definition of excellence? Does what you wrote look more like a daily to-do list than a description of excellence? How clear are you about excellence in your line of work? Ask yourself these questions, continuously, because service suppliers who come to work every day operating from a reference point of excellence produce entirely different outcomes than do employees who take a passive approach to just getting through the day.

It has never been easier to fall into the trap of passivity: Your whole day turns into a series of meetings that don't seem to have anything to do with the most important parts of your job. People with strong brands, however, take a different approach to how they spend their time. They are driven by a standard of excellence and know that having an impact requires making difficult and at times upopular decisions about where they focus their time and attention. They challenge meeting requests and sometimes even the premise for the meeting. They reshape the organization agenda, one meeting at a time, by reframing the dialogue to focus on the truly significant issues, and resist the forces that reinforce the status quo.

Service suppliers also hold themselves directly accountable for business performance, or at least some aspect of it. Their operating belief is that they work in partnership with their organization to attain strong performance. This is a paradigm shift for some, who still see themselves working *for an employer,* which implies a paternalistic relationship where someone will take care of them. These *employees* still think that there is a mysterious *they* to blame for poor business performance or their own job dissatisfaction. The fact is there is no such thing as *they* or *them* in organizations.

There are only many individuals—service suppliers—who work as part of teams that comprise business units that exist to satisfy customers and generate income.

Ironically, *you* may be a *they*. You may be the object of someone else's blame, this blame being a way to divert ownership and accountability. If you're the CEO, some people definitely think of you as a *they*. If you're a manager, you're probably a *they*. People who blame others this way are not empowered and they are not service suppliers.

Do you consider yourself a service supplier? If you do, read on. In the next chapters, you will learn about the 5 P's, a practical methodology for defining, developing, and managing your leadership brand as some of the best service suppliers do. And as you do this, you will also be controlling your destiny at work.

Summary

This chapter introduced the concept of personal and leadership brands, and explained their importance in achieving your goals in your organization. It also set the foundation for thinking about how to continuously manage your brand to control the impression your marketplace has of you. Strong brands are managed, intentional outcomes.

Building a strong brand starts from within—from your own clarity about your unique value for your customers and your business. A hallmark of people who have strong brands is their internal belief that they control their own destiny, and that they are accountable for the impact they have on customers and the bottom line. They take a proactive approach to their work, and don't wait for others to direct them.

You already have a brand, or reputation. Your brand begins in your soul and lands on the street. It's manifested every day in the way others define you and think or speak about you when your name comes up. Just like strong corporate brands, strong personal and leadership brands are rooted in powerful exchanges of genuine value between a service supplier and a buyer. Strong brands are not accidents or flukes. They are the result of focused attention and commitment to a management process. The goal of brand management, then, is to align how you *want* to be understood with how you actually *are* understood.

Developing and owning a strong brand, and marketing it, takes time and it is hard work. It requires a level of focus, discipline, and commitment that *not everyone has*. People who are organization stars aren't passive employees. They are aggressive service suppliers who are willing to put the time, energy, and effort into developing a differentiated exchange of value between themselves and their organizations.

Your Brand Development Plan Worksheet

As you read this book, you will be asked to think about your own brand—understanding it, defining it, developing it, and managing it—and to make notes on your Brand Development Plan Worksheet (a blank Worksheet is provided at the back of the book). After you have finished reading the book, you will have a filled in plan that you can begin to implement immediately to make your brand strong and powerful.

Chapter 2

Persona

All of our guests bring us happiness; some by coming and others by
going.

—Innkeeper's quote

Persona—the first of the 5 P's of Leadership Brand®, is first for a reason.
Organizations are first and foremost social systems. Relationships with co-
workers and customers are paramount to business success.

What Is Persona?

Persona is the emotive, emotional connection and reaction that you elicit
in other people as a result of your personal energy, attitude, style, and
worldview. Persona is all about your ability to effectively connect with
other people and build constructive relationships to get work done.
Persona is a crucial component of your brand value exchange; indeed *it's
the bedrock of your leadership brand.*

As you read this chapter and think about your persona and the reaction
you elicit from your colleagues, keep the innkeeper's quote above in mind.

Persona entails honoring yourself as you are and self-actualizing—not
trying to be someone else. You want to be your best, genuine self, while
being mindful that you work in a highly interdependent social system. The
focus is on you, but you within your market, because of the social nature

of organizations. Your core values, and your ability to regulate your own behaviors and style to get the most out of the situations you face every day at work are the territory of persona. These work situations require *both* content expertise and interpersonal skills. Your inner core as a leader and interpersonal skills as a member of the team become more important as your career progresses. By mid-career, in fact, your interpersonal effectiveness takes on an extraordinarily important role in your success, as your ability to influence others becomes an essential component of getting work done.

The Role of Emotional Intelligence

Emotional intelligence (our ability to recognize and deal with feelings and emotions and to manage them in ourselves and our relationships) is an underpinning of persona. If you don't possess a well-developed level of emotional intelligence, you will encounter significant difficulties managing your brand. Daniel Goleman, a pioneer in the area of emotional intelligence and author of two highly successful books on the subject, found that emotional intelligence is complimentary to the cognitive capacities of IQ. In his book *Working with Emotional Intelligence,* Goleman notes that "In general, emotional competencies play a far larger role in superior job performance than do cognitive abilities and expertise." Unlike IQ, EQ can be taught. When it comes to building a great brand, people in leadership roles know how important it is to work through the personal and professional challenges they face as part of becoming stronger, more self-assured, more inclusive leaders. They possess a balanced, confident combination of self-acceptance, self-awareness, and self-improvement because they have undertaken the necessary developmental efforts involved in acquiring and refining their ability to bring these qualities and capabilities to bear in how they lead. These vital dimensions of emotional intelligence will be explored in-depth later in this chapter.

Let me give you an example of how one successful entrepreneur came to appreciate the profound role emotional intelligence plays in business success. Tina Wells is the founder and CEO of BuzzMarketing Group, a consulting firm providing youth market intelligence to companies including

Sony and Verizon Wireless. Wells, who founded her firm as a teenager and is now in her mid-twenties, says learning the power of persona in business has been very important to her success. "I used to think that my sole objective had to be coming up with the differentiated insights, and the most brilliant thinking on the youth market, and that's where I spent my time," Wells says. "Over time, I started to hear clients say things like, 'what you have to say is really important, but ultimately we decided to go with your firm because we like you.' I realized I had taken a key purchasing dynamic—the ability to relate and really establish a good personal connection—somewhat for granted. It has as much if not more to do with being successful than a one-dimensional focus on bringing great thinking to the table. It paves the way for your thinking to be heard, and for you to influence key business decisions and outcomes."

Wells notes that in her role as CEO, this '*aha*' moment she had earlier in her career has come to make great sense. "I work long hours, at a high level of intensity. Team chemistry is critical. It's not about being able to always agree," Wells says. "In fact it's quite the opposite. We need to be able to agree and disagree, and work through conflict. There's no doubt we do that well because on a fundamental human level, we all like and respect each other on an individual basis. That personal connection motivates us to hear each other out, and to make it work. That's what makes the team so strong."

People have an innate need for affection and connection to others. As social systems, organizations help fill this need. Like Tina Wells, your ability to connect as a manager and leader will directly affect your ability to engender loyalty and excellent performance from employees. In their book *First Break All the Rules,* Marcus Buckingham and Curt Coffman emphasize the important role relationships play in enabling organizations to find and keep top talent. The authors cite twelve questions that form the basis of the Gallup research on what constitutes high performing organizations. One of the questions is, "Does my supervisor, or someone at work, seem to care about me as a person?" The research indicates that a sense of loyalty is engendered when there is an atmosphere of caring and interest from those with whom we work. How well do you connect with others? What data—

from others—do you have to support your conclusions? This second question is important because ensuring that your persona is a healthy, vibrant part of your value exchange means that you have to create productive working relationships *and* have an accurate sense of self. Brands exist in the context of a marketplace, always. Knowing what you intend yours to be is the vital first step, but it's only the first step. It follows that you must know how your intentions "land," that is, how others receive you and whether their perception is aligned with your intentions.

As you can see, gaining clarity about your persona is a process. It begins with learning about yourself and then getting feedback in order to understand how others perceive you. A good place to begin is with the components of persona.

The Components of Persona

Persona is the foundation of all strong brands and it is comprised of the following components: self-awareness, self-confidence, values and vision (persona *within*), and a genuine interest in others that is reflected in well-developed and versatile interpersonal skills (persona *without*). We will explore each of these in detail here, and, later in the chapter, you will read about how one senior manager, Elaine, gained an understanding of her persona.

Self-Awareness

All of us know the difference between people who are self-aware and those who are not. Self-aware people are successful in large part because they know how they come across; they honor emotions and feelings as a legitimate part of business; and they are effective at managing their own emotions and style in social situations. In other words, they are socially skilled. People who lack self-awareness often have a take-me-or-leave-me attitude. Because they don't seem to care about us, we'd prefer to leave them.

It's much more productive to be self-aware, and to develop a persona that creates and manages constructive working relationships with all kinds of people—including those who are different from you. By identifying your vision and values and bringing them to your market in a way that causes others to want to interact with you, this aspect of your persona engages others effectively in pursuit of common goals.

Persona involves being clear about who you are now and who you aspire to be, and how you choose to shape the climate around you based on that self-definition. Your personality and your behavior directly impact your performance, and that of the organization and your colleagues within it. In fact, the preponderance of career derailers—behaviors that can derail your success, or in the extreme, your career—are behavior-based issues that involve how you interact with others. Your ability to authentically and productively connect with other people is vitally important in all human systems, and the business environment is no exception.

Daniel Goleman's research on emotional intelligence reinforces something that most of us already know: your personality plays a major role in your ability to be successful at work. The majority of the executive coaching delivered to businesses in the United States is behavior-based coaching, for this very reason. Creating constructive, productive working relationships with all kinds of people can be complicated and challenging. Doing it successfully requires a strong understanding of self, and of others, and the skills and desire to work through the nuances of interpersonal relationships to achieve productive outcomes. Strong leaders have discovered that understanding their personality more fully is the first step in increasing their self-awareness and emotional intelligence.

Personality Type and Its Role in Self-Awareness

There are numerous ways to increase self-awareness. Many people find it useful to begin with a popular assessment tool developed by two leaders in the field. Isabelle Myers and Katherine Briggs are renowned for their contribution to the literature on personality types. Through their work, we understand the sixteen different personality types (patterns of attitude and outlook, and the actions each type takes as a result) and gain extraordinary insight into who we are and how we think, and into how others think and behave as well. The powerful Myers-Briggs Type Indicator (MBTI) is a personality preference tool used in many venues including career planning and leadership development. It can also be used as a guide to building more solid relationships with others. Unfortunately, in leadership development, this particular tool is over-distributed and underutilized. Most leading business schools in the U.S. ensure that their students undergo the MBTI assessment, but a year later, many cannot recall what they learned. This is true in many organizations as well. Even absent market feedback, these instruments offer vital clues and signals to leaders about their talents and development needs—particularly as they relate to brand persona. Unfortunately, they usually spend more time in the file cabinet than in the dialogue and planning around leadership development.

Personality type tools such as MBTI enable us to understand the origins of our strengths and areas for development based on our innate natural preferences—in many ways how we see and interface with the world around us. For example, we know that some personality types value the pursuit of knowledge and accumulation of knowledge above building relationships and are apt to develop relationships as a secondary function to their primary goals; we sometimes experience these individuals as less socially concerned. In its extreme, this type may receive brand data to the effect that, "he gets great results but leaves a trail of dead bodies behind him." Others achieve fulfillment in just the opposite way—through a primary emphasis on development of personal connections—and work to help others grow through affirmation and praise. In the extreme, this type might be criticized for a reluctance or inability to "provide the balanced picture and critically analyze the logic, or find the flaws." Neither is right or wrong, and the intention of this brief discussion is to illustrate the direct and powerful influence that our core, hard-wired personality has on our brand persona.

As you read about persona, you may in fact be actively making judgments about the degree to which you think social skills, and relationship development and management *really* matter (in spite of my strong opinion) based on your own personality preferences. Your views are driven by your underlying values—about what's truly important. The point is we don't all think alike, nor do we ascribe value to the same things.

Uniqueness is the key to a strong brand, but there are persona-related dynamics that all leaders need to consider. Great brands—and certainly the brands of true leaders—are first developed inside the individual; they live from the inside out. They begin with your character: who you are and what you stand for. They include your energy, attitude, world view and preferred style—and can be illuminated through tools like MBTI. But they don't end there. Like all brands, yours exists in the context of your marketplace. It's not enough to know who you are and how you operate; your real task is to know how to take that awareness and work with it to be effective in the social system in which you provide services. Self-awareness is the key to knowing how to adjust your style to be effective.

Social Isolation and the Narcissistic Leader

Organizations work best when the members in them connect and communicate effectively. And yet, some leaders deploy a personal style that prevents healthy social connection and communication from occurring. Sometimes, the person preventing it isn't even aware he's doing it. One manifestation of this operating style has been captured in Michael Maccoby's work on narcissistic leadership. The narcissistic leader's characteristics include excessive love or admiration of oneself, self-preoccupation, lack of empathy, and unconscious deficits in self-esteem. These leaders can be quite charming and can engage large teams in pursuit of breakthrough results. Although well-appreciated for the passion they bring to achieving stretch goals and grand visions, narcissistic leaders' excessive self-orientation, and creation of climates where no one dares criticize them, can lead to dysfunctional teams, one-sided relationships, and the downfall of the business and its leader because he or she is isolated from vital information and feedback.

The social isolation of narcissistic leaders prohibits their giving and getting helpful feedback, which also negatively affects individual and organizational growth. Ironically, taking the risk to obtain and work through the feedback would enhance their confidence and increase their effectiveness.

Social isolation can also result from a leader's intensity of focus, sharp edge, dismissive attitude, or fiery temper, and it has direct implications for the organization's climate and others' willingness to take risks. In one company whose hot-tempered CEO was the stuff of legend, senior managers recounted with great clarity the various times they had been the subject of the CEO's ire—often in public—and that experience taught them to act with great caution and care, which translated into lost opportunities for individuals and the organization.

Every leader must create a climate where open, constructive feedback is the norm, because it is a critical enabler of sustainable market leadership. Whether intimidating or intimidated, leaders who discourage productive communication find that self-isolation is the result in either case. Climates of fear are untenable and the leaders who create them don't last. Climates characterized by dishonest or incomplete communication are always at risk because the voice of the market—the ultimate determinant of demand—is squelched. The personas of leaders are at the very center of the climate of their teams or entire enterprises.

Self-Confidence

Self-confidence is the second component of every leader's persona, and feedback again plays a vital role in it. The ability to seek and obtain honest feedback on a regular basis is for many—regardless of race, gender, or culture—an acquired taste. Strong brands are owned by strong people, and these people all began their journey with different levels of self-confidence. It is ultimately self-confidence, and the comfort of knowing we are not perfect, nor can we ever be, that sets up the foundation for genuine and accurate self-awareness, and the commitment to self-improvement that follows. Building a core of true self-confidence is not easy, and for some it's an extraordinarily difficult task that takes place over many years.

One way to work toward greater self-confidence is to begin taking thoughtful risks, one at a time, starting small. *Syndicate* your risk by engaging others upstream and obtaining their input, buy-in and support. Reflect on each risk experience, learn from what happened, and step out to take the next one. (This process works for building self-awareness through feedback as well, since soliciting feedback takes a measure of courage. In Chapter 7 you will learn how to collect market feedback on your brand

and develop a keen awareness of how well your intentions are aligned with your market's reality, or perceptions.) *Embracing Fear* by Thom Rutledge offers an insightful treatment of how to build self-confidence. Intelligent risk-taking and self-confidence are recurring themes in this book because they are prerequisites to business success today, and therefore the purview of strong leadership brands.

Values and Vision

As managers of our own brands, we have to continually pursue our highest vision of who we can be. We're fully accountable for that, and no one else can or should do it for us. Allowing others to dictate who you *should be* never brings the same happiness, success, and self-actualization that working through it yourself, on your own terms, does.

Implementing your values and vision requires self-confidence. All of us know people who try to be someone they're not and this is often rooted in their lack of confidence to be who they are. Imagine the disastrous results that would ensue if a company behaved this way, and wasn't clear about its values and its brands. David Aaker, an expert on consumer brand management, calls this "customer orientation gone amok." In his book *Building Strong Brands,* Aaker writes, "It's like the cartoon where a market researcher arrives at a nearly finished Sistine Chapel to say, 'Personally, I think it looks OK, Michelangelo, but the focus group says it needs more mauve.' Creating a brand identity is more than finding out what customers say they want. It must also reflect the soul and vision of the brand, what it hopes to achieve."

As you build and manage your brand, your soul (your values) and your vision must be centermost in your pursuit of your career goals. Successful, happy people everywhere know this secret. This focus on your values and vision will ensure that you have the necessary alignment—the direct line that connects your inner vision and values with your ability to *create* value at your organization. An example of this alignment in action is Ann Fudge, whose distinguished career to date includes leadership roles at Kraft Foods and as CEO of Young & Rubicam. When she was named CEO of Y&R, her values, vision, and self-confidence were described in an interview with

Bob Eckert, Chairman and CEO of Mattel, who was Fudge's boss when she was at Kraft Foods: "She interacts effectively with all constituencies; is equally comfortable with consumers at the ballpark, factory workers on a production line, and executives in the boardroom. She's very comfortable with herself and not pretending to be someone else. That's what makes her such an effective leader."

A personal vision is a powerful thing, and it is part of your brand signature. Do you have a personal vision for yourself? A picture of how you see the world? Of how your business could be significantly better five or ten years from now? Do you have this kind of dream? It's your big picture aspiration for your own future, and of your future as you lead your organization forward. Bringing your best self to work means bringing your *aligned* self, the self who's clear about vision, values, beliefs, attitudes toward self and work, and the experience others have of you.

Great leaders have two things in common: They live by a standard of excellence, and they are guided by their own clear vision of a better future. They embody a powerful combination of confidence, tenacity, steadiness, and purpose. Do you know people with these qualities? Are you one of them? Vision and purpose are very powerful devices that enable leaders to focus, prioritize, and let go of the trivial in pursuit of the grand. More importantly, vision and purpose enable you to move from self-focus to market-focus, and this shift brings breakthroughs for you and your organization.

Interpersonal Skills

Three examples illustrate the importance of interpersonal skills, which affect how other people perceive us every day at work (our marketplace) in a thousand small ways. The first involves Harry, a division finance executive. Late one night, as Harry is sitting in his office going through his inbox, his phone rings. As he reaches to answer it, he glances at the caller ID and sees that the incoming call is from Bob. His hand stops in mid-air, and he refrains from picking up the receiver. He lets the phone ring and goes back to his reading. Bob's call goes unanswered. Why? "It's not that I mind the interruption," Harry says. "It's that I mind who the interruption is from. Bob just has a way of operating that grates on my nerves—his tone, his edge of sarcasm, the way he grouses about his teammates. He's irritating. I don't know how else to explain it other than to say it's a turn-off working with him so I tend to avoid him when I can." Bob's persona elicits a negative visceral reaction by the hundreds of small things he says and does. This, in turn, has an ongoing detrimental effect on him and his ability to achieve on behalf of his organization and its customers.

As noted, the ability to build relationships and establish rapport with all kinds of people is essential to persona, and to strong leadership. As a second example, imagine that a meeting is held with a dozen or so people who are selecting the project leader and team members for an upcoming high profile project. One by one, the names of individuals in the organization are presented as possible candidates. One of those names is yours. When your name is mentioned, what's the visceral reaction of those in the room? What do they say to themselves about you? Do they think, "Hmmmmm, he's a terrific guy; I've heard a lot of great things about him—he brings real vision to his work and is respected as a team player"? Or, do they groan and say, "Oh no; not her. She's so high maintenance—I heard she drove everybody on her last project away with her 'in your face' approach. Plus, there are some real trust issues with her." In most organizations, what gets shared out loud is a mere shadow of the real thought, toned down to fit organizational communication norms. Note that these negatives are values-driven (trustworthiness, respect for others, social integrity) and are aspects of persona that start from within the individual.

The third scenario occurs when two or more candidates are being considered for an assignment. If they are seen as equally skilled, the selection will likely default to an aspect of persona, that is, which one do I, as the hiring manager, connect best with? Which one do I trust? Which one will best represent the team and drive our value exchange forward?

The importance of establishing that connection, that interpersonal rapport that facilitates getting work done, can't be overstated. (You'll see how important it is when you read the real-world example of Elaine's story later.) The ability to influence others is an increasingly important skill in business where cross-functional collaboration is required. Influencing skills—the ability to gain support for ideas and their implementation from people over whom you have no formal authority—require solid interpersonal skills, a key aspect of persona.

With Persona, Perception Is Reality

Because persona is the core of your leadership brand, you're accountable for knowing how you are perceived, and then for actively managing your style to ensure your exchanges with others are positive and productive. Does that mean you have to pander to others and work to win personality contests? Absolutely not. Does it mean the "I am who I am, they can take it or leave it" attitude is an abdication of personal responsibility? Yes. Does it mean you need to possess the self-awareness, self-assurance, and self-discipline to accurately read others' reaction to you and, where prudent, modify your behavior accordingly? Absolutely. Your success depends on it.

As we know, organizations are inherently social, and they run on relationships. Each organization's rules and norms around social style and behavior are unwritten and unique, but every organization has them. One unwritten rule around persona, for example, is that as you ascend, you are expected to balance your hard-driving style with an ability to build, maintain and, where necessary, mend relationships with all levels of the organization, especially the executive team. Another is that women who are hard-driving and aggressive are more apt to receive feedback to polish that edge than are men. Successful women executives who have received that feedback know they don't have to give up the traits that made them successful, but they do have to be more sophisticated in how they work with others to achieve shared goals. Other's perceptions are indeed their own reality; adjusting your style to increase your impact and effectiveness can only be done right when you know how you are showing up to others.

Regardless of gender, as you advance closer to the top of the organization, your ability to develop collegial, trusting relationships with other senior leaders is a cost of admission to the executive suite. And why wouldn't this be true? The CEO and top leadership team of most organizations are under extraordinary pressure to perform, to make the right decisions under significant stress and time constraints, and to grow profits in a rapidly consolidating global marketplace. These people work together seventy or eighty hours a week at the office, conferences, and at evening and weekend events. Given these scenarios, wouldn't *you* surround yourself with highly competent people you respect and with whom you have rapport?

Getting Persona Feedback and Creating Your Action Plan

Now let's apply what you've learned about persona. What are aspects of your persona that you consider strengths? Aspects that you think may need some work to ensure you're as effective as possible? As you read the following tips and advice, make notes on the Brand Development Plan Worksheet that you started when you read the Introduction to this book. (Elaine's story will also be the source of some ideas.) Remember, sometimes our greatest strengths, when overdone, become weaknesses in need of improvement.

Ask for and Act on Feedback

I can't over-emphasize the importance of getting quality feedback as you develop your brand through the many components of persona (and as you fill in your Worksheet). Remember, perception is reality, and if you are going to take charge of your own impact and career, you must understand how others perceive you.

For example, a senior executive recently shared some important thoughts on leadership at a national sales meeting of his organization. He said that a leader's effectiveness is in part a function of how he or she spends time, noting that too many leaders "starve stars" while "feeding weak performers." Where is your focus as a leader in this regard? What might that say about you and your abilities? What might it suggest about your leadership brand? Are you aware of how you are perceived?

Are you yourself perceived as a star, a "B" player, or a weak performer? If you have been coached or counseled by your manager to improve an aspect of your work—intellectual or behavioral—take it seriously. Instead of responding defensively (placing blame with your manager and others), focus hard on addressing the shortfall. Ask for feedback from your manager. Show that you care. Meet agreed-upon deadlines. Doing so gets you back into alignment with your market around your intentions; not doing so exacerbates the focus on the misalignment.

Don't Blame the Ref

Perhaps you spend much of your non-working time as I do: driving your kids to soccer, basketball, tennis, football, etc. Over the years, we've developed a ground rule for the inevitable post-game conversation that takes place on the way home in the car: *If you have a bad game, don't blame the referee*. That rule has made the game post-mortem more constructive, and it can do the same at work. Focus on what you can control and how you can make things better. Imagine what would happen if you brought your game up to the next level. Don't blame the ref—if you do this, you give away all your power and position yourself as a grouser who saps the energy of the team.

This doesn't mean that on occasion there aren't unfair or bad calls. For example, the unlevel playing field for women and people of color in Corporate America plays itself out in many ways, one of which is the lack of access to executives (often white males) at the top of the organization. Sometimes my clients describe themselves as "the only" woman or person of color at a high level. They say that a lack of access to senior executives affects their development and mobility by limiting exposure to teaching, mentoring, information, and casual opportunities for connecting and relationship building. The "access gap" can also play a role in selection, when someone who is less well known loses out to a candidate who already has a working relationship (and, thus, an established brand) with the hiring executive. While brand management is important for every professional and executive, women and people of color have learned that using the 5 P's framework to manage their brands with even greater rigor and discipline is indeed a way to close this access gap and bring some leveling to the playing field. But it *is* controllable; abdicating personal responsibility for effective leadership brand management amounts to giving up control over outcomes that are, in fact, very much in our own control. Blaming the ref is tantamount to taking ourselves out of the game.

Multiple Personality Syndrome

In every workshop I've conducted, at least one participant is confused by conflicting market feedback. "My staff experiences me one way, while others see me differently. What do I do with this information? Which one is right?" The answer is both, because perception is reality. Having multiple personalities may or may not be a problem. If your communication style is direct and to the point with senior management, for example, but less structured and more loose with staff reporting to you, it's probably working well. If you are two different people *altogether,* depending on your environment, you've got a problem. Here are two examples.

Example 1

Feedback from staff:

"One of the finest managers I've ever worked for."
"Takes our individual needs into account better than anyone."
"Really works to know us."
"Has my loyalty forever."

Feedback from senior management:

"Don't see her taking ownership when things go wrong."
"Is in constant need of praise—it takes all the energy out of our team meetings."
"Where she doesn't step up to own mistakes, you always wonder if there's going to be surprise bad news."
"Has a bit of that Ronald Reagan 'Teflon' to her. Nothing seems to stick."

Example 2

Feedback from staff:

"He has very little time for us—it seems his focus is all about managing up."

Feedback from senior management:

"He's a terrific communicator and really strong performer. On the short list for promotion and to run a larger organization."

In both of these examples, the individual is experiencing the downside of multiple personality syndrome. In the first example, the individual is working from a comfort zone that centers on downward management to her staff, but she is not working effectively with senior management. Her feedback is a reflection of her need to build confidence dealing with senior management, and to assume a more direct and realistic approach to communicating with them.

In the second example, the opposite is true. This individual's feedback indicates that his focus on managing up, which he no doubt found to be considerably more interesting than managing sideways or down, is negatively impacting his brand because he is not meeting the expectations of his team.

The degree to which persona plays into the overall strength of your brand has to do with how much emphasis your particular marketplace assigns to relationship development and maintenance. All of the organizations I work with—from financial services to publishing to biotechnology—place some measure of value on relationships; most place *significant* value on them. Therefore, people with strong brands typically score moderately to very high in persona. Persona is especially important in organizations that genuinely value service providers who consistently act in accordance with key values such as integrity, teamwork, and customer focus. Leaders in these organizations are aware of the powerful effect of their personas on their value exchanges, and they actively manage their personas to assure their continued success.

A third way multiple personality syndrome plays out for leaders is that they are rated very favorably in interpersonal skills and overall relationship management, but only by those with whom they are comfortable. This can translate into leaders who create a climate of welcome for others most like them, but who either struggle to do so or choose not to invest in doing the same for those who are less like them, based on gender, race, or even personal style. Unless accountabilities are built into the performance management system, this can go unchecked. The great cost is to the organization, which never reaps the benefits of the talents and capabilities of these other players, and therefore loses its market edge. Talented, ambitious players of both genders and all colors don't typically wait around to be marginalized; rather they leave and find an organization where they can contribute fully.

Actively Manage Your Relationship with Your Boss

We have thus far explored the role persona plays as you manage your on-going impact in your organization. But there is another situation in which persona has a crucial impact: downsizing.

Sometimes when employees are notified that their positions have been eliminated, they say, "I wasn't that surprised…my manager and I just don't get along." In truth, very few people get along perfectly with their managers. But strong boss-subordinate relationships or relationships with colleagues are the product of on-going effort by all parties involved.

Layoffs—whether they are due to economic downturn, corporate restructuring, globalization of the business, or outsourcing of business functions—are here to stay. There are some employees who are at greater risk in difficult economic times, and the irony is they often put themselves at greater risk because they choose not to regulate and manage highly controllable aspects of their persona—their attitude, energy, and style, and the need to invest in managing up.

How you manage your relationship with your manager—directly and indirectly—is quite important and completely within your control. All of us have encountered someone who publicly grouses about his or her manager ("She just doesn't get it" or "He's so clueless"). Somehow these comments find their way to the manager—because organizations are social systems and they thrive on story-telling. A misstep like this often becomes someone else's opportunity. Later that day, week, month or quarter, that same manager is told to reduce staff. Put yourself in the manager's shoes. If you can't trust a team member to perform and reflect positively on others in the good times, why would you want that person hanging around in high-risk employment periods? Negativity is dangerous because it creates mistrust, and trust is central to strong relationships and strong brands. Once the bonds of trust are broken, rebuilding them is extremely difficult. The better alternative is direct, honest, one-to-one communication that reflects a well-developed brand persona and leads to constructive, positive, and lasting outcomes.

Let's look at an example of how one person, Elaine, developed an action plan for managing her persona. As you read, look for ways to use Elaine's insight to add to your own Persona Action Plan.

Elaine's Story: Persona in Action

Elaine's Persona Feedback

Feedback is essential to professional development and to understanding your brand, and it will be explored in greater detail in Chapter 7, including what to obtain and how to obtain it. But for now, in order to understand persona, we will look at an example of feedback about Elaine, who is a senior sales manager at a pharmaceuticals firm. (Elaine's name, position, and industry are fictitious.)

In this example, Elaine has gotten in-depth feedback on her leadership brand through work she has undertaken with an executive coach. As part of the assessment process in the coaching, Elaine's coach conducted one-on-one interviews with a set of Elaine's stakeholders—colleagues, subordinates, and her boss and several senior executives—and brought that feedback to Elaine for analysis and action planning. Elaine has analyzed her feedback by answering a series of questions, including:

- What are the dominant strengths of my brand—my brand attributes?
- What are the drags on my brand—the characteristics of it that create friction and slow me down from getting to my ideal?
- Under which of the 5 P's do the attributes and drags fall?
- What's the essence of my exchange of value with my marketplace, and how strong is it?

Let's take a look at what the data reveal about Elaine.

Brand Element: Persona	Brand Attributes	Brand Drags
Communication	Direct, crisp, and to the point	Gets great results but can give debilitating feedback—only the strong survive. Lacks patience at times.
Work style	Results-orientation	Doesn't build relationships with peers.
Focus	'No-nonsense' style	Can focus on the business at the expense of the relationship—won't win in the long run that way.

Interpreting Elaine's feedback

As an executive coach who helps clients develop strategies to improve their effectiveness, I frequently have the opportunity to work with senior managers whose hard-driving, results-orientation is overdone. These are bright, talented leaders who become stuck because they have taken for granted or underinvested in building constructive relationships with other key players. These relationships are essential to getting work done—especially difficult and controversial work. They are often quite surprised to discover how important relationships and interpersonal dynamics are, and to learn the extent to which they affect work outcomes.

Elaine's persona data indicate that her strengths are her no-nonsense, to-the-point style, and her ability to engender loyalty from her team. While quite significant, these attributes can sometimes be limiting, as we see when we read across to the drags column. Brand drags are aspects of an individual's brand that are seen as creating friction, or as slowing the individual down from reaching a goal or achieving an ideal brand.

Brand drags may include missing or weak skills, or skills that are poorly applied. Interestingly, as people move along in their careers, they are apt to see their strengths show up on their brand analysis as both strengths *and* weaknesses. A brand may suffer because a strength is used to excess, or used in the wrong venue. One person, for example, may appreciate a very direct and to-the-point communication style, while another may be put on the defensive by that same approach. Elaine's persona feedback is typical for ascending professionals with Elaine's results-driven style.

Elaine's persona drags paint a picture of a sales manager who has a near-singular focus on results, and who views her work in a fairly narrow frame. The feedback indicates she defines her work through a vertical frame—her people and her numbers—and despite her success in this area, her market is telling her that this approach is problematic. Interestingly, this is a relatively new development for Elaine. The message from Elaine's marketplace is that, because she's no longer an *aspiring* sales manager but a *senior* sales manager, she needs to expand her frame of reference to see the whole field and not simply operate from her position within it. While a narrow view of her role and her world may have been appropriate on her way up—in fact may have been the approach she needed to be successful—it is no longer acceptable or effective given her level of scope and responsibility. It is now a limiting view, which, if not corrected, will undermine her value exchange and ultimately marginalize her.

From a brand development perspective, Elaine's first step is to redefine her central work to include building relationships with a wider set of stakeholders. She needs to shift her frame of reference from the vertical (with her team, where relationships are clearly strong) to the horizontal, creating and maintaining working relationships with a broader range of peers and stakeholders, and with a frame of reference that extends across the enterprise. Further, the texture of the relationships with peers and those senior to Elaine needs to change from being exclusively task-based (acceptable and appropriate for someone more junior) to a style that melds that task focus with a warmer, more personal, conversational approach. At mid-level and above, the interpersonal relationships become the foundation that supports the task-based work. They also form the basis for the coalitions and alliances necessary to influence and drive the business in new directions.

Elaine's reaction to this feedback might include the frustration she associates with "wasting time on the fluff." She might say, "Why can't people just focus on the work? I have a huge job, a family, and a lot to do. I don't have time in my day for useless chit chat." In these words, Elaine is actually providing important insight into who she is and what she values. It also linked directly to what she had learned about her leadership style through her Myers-Briggs assessment. This is quite significant because it hits at her core beliefs and the operating and personal style that she has developed out of those beliefs. Nonetheless, she will need to rethink the importance of the interpersonal side of the work. Developing a modified approach in this area will not be an easy task for Elaine. Her success modifying her personal style will depend on how much she believes this style affects her ability to perform and grow in her career.

Creating Elaine's Persona Action Plan

A sample action plan for Elaine's persona would address three main areas for improvement: building relationships with others, adding a brief social component at the beginning of interpersonal exchanges, and softening her direct communication style. Of course, this assumes that Elaine has decided that she genuinely *wants* to invest in building relationships; otherwise she won't succeed.

A good way for Elaine to begin to build relationships would be to create opportunities over coffee, dinner, or golf (or its equivalent) to develop closer relationships with selected stakeholders. Her plan should span at least a twelve-month period. In the beginning, these activities can be quite stressful for someone with Elaine's style. ("What in the world will we talk about if it's not related to Project X?") In the early phase of implementation, the key is to prepare ahead of time. Elaine could begin by asking herself questions: What are this person's interests? Which of my interests would I enjoy talking about? What do we have in common? The key is to identify a few areas of conversation that will help Elaine and the other person get to know each other and find areas of common interest. (I've seen this work effectively for a client of mine who was pleasantly surprised to learn over dinner that a business partner, whom he'd known for years, shared his great interest in American inventors. They had a terrific conversation, used it to build on their relationship, and created a much stronger foundation on which to get their work done.)

The second piece of Elaine's action plan should focus on building a brief social component upfront in all the interpersonal exchanges she has each day at work—at the beginning of phone calls, the start of meetings, and even chance encounters in the hallway or elevator. She could simply take a few moments to inquire with genuine interest about other people by asking how their weekend was and why, by sharing a complaint about the morning commute, and by following up with a question based on what people share ("Oh, have you lived on the North Shore long?"). In other words, be brief, but be real, and then get to work.

The third brand drag that Elaine's action plan needs to address is her direct communication style. Clearly, some individuals appreciate Elaine's direct feedback and work with it quite well; these are probably people whose style is similar to Elaine's. But because organizations need to attract, retain, and develop people with diverse styles, it will be important for Elaine, and all leaders, to ensure that their personas help, rather than hinder, this process. Elaine's third key area of development, then, is to change how she communicates and provides feedback to ensure that she is building—not destroying—the confidence of other important team members. In this situation, leaders often find the *plus/delta* feedback model extremely helpful. This is a simple, straightforward tool that helps people get into the habit of providing constructive feedback in a two-step process: First, begin with what worked (the plus), followed by your thoughts on what could be done differently or better next time (the delta). People with Elaine's direct style find this model useful because it helps them control their habit of immediately criticizing the person, his actions, or his ideas. It helps reshape the dialogue in two important ways: It begins the discussion with something positive, which reaffirms the other person's sense of self, and it follows with recommended improvements, but not in the damning language of "what you did wrong." Previously, Elaine would have given feedback this way: "You really handled that question on the revenue shortfall poorly. You were defensive and it showed. It didn't reflect well on you." Elaine's work, then, will focus on using language that helps build, not tear down, the other person's sense of competence and confidence.

By getting feedback and developing her action plan, Elaine now has a blueprint for building a strong persona that will help her achieve her organizational and individual goals. The improved relationships that she builds will be based on open communication and mutual respect and, thus, will create an environment where people feel comfortable disagreeing, raising concerns, and bringing alternatives and new ideas forward.

Summary

Brand management has as its guiding principle honoring and self-actualizing each individual. Great brands are first developed inside the individual; they live from the inside out.

Your persona is the emotive, emotional connection and reaction that you elicit in other people as a result of your personal energy, attitude, style, and worldview. It can be a powerful ally or enemy to your goals and self-interest, and can also affect the energy, attitude, and ultimately the organization as a whole.

Persona is comprised of four components: self-awareness, self-confidence, values and vision, and interpersonal skills. Perception is reality, so it is up to you to learn how you are perceived—to understand the degree to which your intentions are in fact aligned with others' reality—and to do what's necessary to ensure your exchanges with others are positive and productive. The best way to do this is to get feedback from your market-place (and especially your manager) on an ongoing basis. Feedback is essential for your professional development and to understand your brand.

The importance of establishing rapport to facilitate getting work done cannot be overstated. Along with rapport, the ability to influence others is an increasingly important skill in business.

Update your Brand Development Plan Worksheet now

Take a moment to identify action areas that belong in the persona section of your brand development worksheet at the back of this book. Look again at the four components of persona and make some notes about others' perceptions of your brand in these areas. How do you rate your own emotional quotient (your EQ?) Do you know your personality type and do you use this knowledge to understand your strengths and areas for development. Are there some changes you need to make to ensure a strong brand?

Chapter 3

Product

You probably own at least one piece of wheeled carry-on luggage; most of us do. The popularity of this particular kind of suitcase did not escape Consumer Reports®, which recently tested a series of models for its readers. When Consumer Reports® tests a product for quality, the tests are both rigorous and comprehensive. In evaluating this class of suitcases, for example, testers navigate the same Consumer Reports-designed obstacle course with each bag loaded with fifty pounds of weight. The course includes carpeted floor, smooth tile, and concrete, as well as prototypes of rough pavement and even sewer grates. There's a portion of the course that includes figure eights, high curbs, and S-turns. Then the bag is tossed into a machine resembling a giant clothes dryer where it is tumbled over and over about 1,000 times. By the time the testing is over, there is no doubt about which products are genuinely high quality and which are not.

In managing your own brand, do you continuously scrutinize the quality and capacity of your product—your skills, intellect, and track record built through them—as rigorously as Consumer Reports® tests carry-on luggage? How does your product compare on the basis of value to other suppliers of similar services? What is the basis for your analysis and comparison? The smart wheeled luggage manufacturers have no doubt how their product will test under the scrutiny of Consumer Reports® because they've run their suitcase through their own rigorous analysis long before Consumer Reports® selects the luggage for testing. These manufacturers prefer being their own toughest critic, knowing that controlling product quality is their responsibility and that the alternative—leaving it to the chance scrutiny of others in their marketplace—is a very risky business proposition. Leaving it to chance gives away power, leaves interpretation of quality and value to others, and may ultimately result in an unwelcome surprise.

What Is Product?

Product is all about substance. Your substance. It is the sum of your professional qualifications, experience, technical and/or functional expertise, and results you've delivered over time. It includes your track record of homeruns, your failed efforts, and how you process those experiences to sharpen your skills.

This chapter explores specific aspects of brand product in the context of evolving from an individual contributor into a leader of increasingly large teams and businesses. But having a successful product is also dependent upon *fit,* or making sure you are in the right job and organization. Fit plays a powerful role in career success and one's sense of self-esteem and is an important contributor to a healthy product. In his book *Please Understand Me II*, David Keirsey notes that professionals sometimes seem to have "Peter Principled" (to have reached their own level of incompetence in the organization) when, in fact, they may be highly competent but simply in the wrong job. I've seen this happen to people who are fabulous individual contributors when they accept promotions into jobs managing others because they see this as the only way to advance. As you work to continuously enhance your exchange of value with your organization, it's important to ask yourself whether the next opportunity will leverage your core strengths and be a positive stretch, or whether you may not have the inclination or capacity to excel in it. Establish and use your own board of directors to get honest feedback as part of your deliberations.

From Individual Contributor to Manager to Leader

The figure below presents a continuum depicting the progression of one's value exchange from individual contributor to manager to leader. There are a number of capabilities that provide the lift needed to support movement toward leadership, but one is essential: the ability to delegate. (We'll read more about this later.) It is the competency that enables managers to grow into leaders, to engender loyalty by enabling team members to develop, and to encourage creative thinking, innovating, and risk-taking among top talent.

Continuous Development of Your Value Exchange Over Time

Individual Contributor	**Manager** **"Results-getter"**	**Leader**
Focus:	Focus:	Focus:
Self	My team	The entire team
Specific task or project	Oversight	Broad direction
Meeting "deliverable"	Meeting "deliverable"	Creating value
Solo performance	"On task, on time"	Innovation

This shift from detail or tactics to big picture and strategy is easier for some than others. The detail-oriented person, whose proficiency with detail has been the source of his or her success, may have difficulty letting go of that orientation to grow into a big picture player. It is also a challenge for people with a high need for control. The issues of detail orientation and control often come up in development discussions when an experienced manager is being asked to take it to the next level and lead with greater impact and intention. Frequently, such a manager will say, "I don't know what that means. If I'm not doing the work, then what *is* my work?" But as you'll see later in this chapter, learning to delegate is an essential part of being a strong leader. In fact, delegation is a key component of a strong product.

Determining Your Fit

Perhaps you don't want to go from individual contributor to manager to leader. Maybe you have determined that your strengths and passions lie in the technical or specialist areas. Should you ignore that calling because you think you should pursue a leadership role in spite of your interests and skills? Of course not. Remember what we said earlier about the link between the right fit and successful performance.

As you work on your product, your responsibility is to know yourself extremely well—to know what your core strengths are and embrace and value them—and to direct yourself toward your interests and passions, creating a powerful value exchange from that base. Your best fit may be in a technical or specialist area, or managing a small group of sophisticated professionals in an internal consulting capacity.

Whatever your official title, however, intellectual growth is requisite to a strong value exchange. Monitor the key components of your value exchange: What innovations have you introduced? How broadly do you reach across the organization to engage others in solutions-generation? How have you and your team improved efficiencies? Improved core processes? Made your business measurably more competitive? By holding yourself accountable to these outcomes, you are taking on a leadership role regardless of your title or place in the hierarchy. Next we will turn to the main elements of a strong product.

The Components of Product

Product is the second key input (after persona) into your differentiated value exchange. For leaders, product has four components: a strategic frame of reference, continuous learning, the ability to delegate and grow talent, and risk-taking and innovation. Let's look at each one in more detail. Later in this chapter, we will see how Elaine obtained feedback on each of her product components and how she used that feedback to take specific actions that enhanced her product in her marketplace.

Strategic Frame of Reference

There's an old German proverb that says, "What's the sake of running if you are not on the right road?" Achieving your business and career goals requires you to have both a targeted outcome and a strategy to get there. Your strategy is the game plan you develop in order to achieve your vision and objectives. It's the approach that results in differentiated performance, for the business and for your own leadership brand.

Solid strategies begin with a big picture understanding of where the business is trying to go, where the opportunities are, and what's required to seize them. Even as you read this, stop for a moment: are you able to articulate where your business—not just your business *unit* but the entire organization—needs to be in three or five years? What changes will be necessary for it to get there? What are the most urgent issues and opportunities facing your organization today? How must it change to compete? A *manager*—especially a results-getter in overdrive—is likely to leave that question to others; a *leader* is likely to be thinking that through continuously, even if she or he is not the CEO. Good strategists always have a game plan, but are able and willing to modify it in the face of compelling new developments. Men are also more likely to both hold and offer opinions in this regard than are women, and yet doing this kind of thinking and expressing your point of view on it is fundamental to owning a strong product. Clearly the message to women leaders and emerging leaders is to hold yourself accountable for thinking like the CEO, long before you become one.

As you move through your career, your organization expects you to build increasingly sophisticated strategic approaches to address new issues and seize new opportunities. You enhance your value exchange by moving from the order-taker mode (appropriate earlier in your career), to order-giver mode as you increasingly hold yourself accountable for reading market dynamics and creating solutions to address them. You begin this process by demonstrating your ability to move from a vertical to horizontal frame intellectually and in your relationships and networks. This ability helps you grow and take a more holistic view of the business and its challenges and opportunities. You are able to adjust your line of sight across functions, then across lines of business, and ultimately across and beyond the entire enterprise. As you do this, you look for new opportunities that can translate into business growth. With this increasingly wide frame of reference, you are able to devise a plan that will help you reach your goals, using all the levers and resources at your disposal. A great strategy differentiates the business, which, in turn, differentiates the leadership brand of the strategist, i.e., you.

Continuous Learning

Continuous learning is the cornerstone of long-term strength in product. Without a commitment in this area, the risk of stalling in your career increases, and you will essentially be taking yourself out of the game for promotions and interesting assignments.

While management and leadership are related, they are not the same thing. In *The Seven Habits of Highly Effective People,* author Stephen Covey says, "The leader is the one who climbs the tallest tree, surveys the entire situation, and yells, 'Wrong jungle!' But how do the busy, efficient producers and managers often respond? 'Shut up! We're making progress.'"

In his extensive work on leadership and in his book *Learning to Lead,* Warren Bennis describes leadership as "influencing, guiding in direction, course, action, opinion." In today's flatter organizations, managers may also be leaders, and leaders may also be managers, depending on the situation.

Leaders think futuristically as part of their role as strategist. They see possibilities and opportunities, and from that vantage point create powerful and compelling visions of a better future. Their sense of hope and optimism for the future (rooted in their unique persona) enables them to engage and inspire others to actively and collaboratively participate in helping the business fulfill that vision.

John F. Kennedy said, "Leadership and learning are indispensable." In order to sustain your value exchange over the life of your career, it is essential to develop the leadership qualities described above. The business needs your best thinking, which includes harnessing all of your experience and lessons learned, and bringing them to bear on new problems and opportunities. Your own commitment to continuous learning is key to ensuring that your value exchange remains robust. Assignments that offer a broad view of the organization and its marketplace are a great way to learn. Executives who have taken these broad assignments to round out their capabilities have discovered that they are not without risk, however. These assignments typically require leaving the P&L environment, where executives may have built a strong reputation and are comfortable with their success, and entering an unknown part of the business in order to broaden their perspective and develop a multidimensional outlook.

But before you consider such an assignment, it's helpful to create an inventory of your product-based skills and capabilities to discover the essence of your current value exchange. Sharing this inventory with others who are familiar with your work, including your personal board of directors, can provide insight into your blind spots. An inventory will show you at a glance your strengths *and* areas of vulnerability requiring focused improvement.

In addition to volunteering for challenging assignments within the organization, successful mid-career players are usually active in industry roundtables and other senior-level forums where they often develop personal relationships with powerful, influential mentors and peers to accelerate their learning. These forums also stimulate new thinking, and assure that you are exposed in a timely manner to ideas and best practices that you can bring back to your organization marketplace. Managers and leaders who are actively managing their brands invest the time and money necessary to attend these forums, while their colleagues, who may be stuck in *results-getter* mode are back at the office with their heads down in their work, less focused on the important role continuous learning plays in their advancement.

Ability to Delegate and Grow Talent

Emerging leaders often find that, as senior management is pushing them to transition from managers to leaders, their staff still wants them to provide technical guidance and be a sounding board on technical issues. The staff doesn't feel safe with a manager who isn't superior to them technically. What's the right balance to strike with these competing demands? Because the organization needs leaders who can mobilize diverse individuals and groups in pursuit of the strategy, senior managers will rarely press emerging leaders to build technical expertise at the expense of developing leadership skills, strategic acumen, systems thinking, and the other competencies that enable the leader to lead. Paul Hogan, former vice chairman at FleetBoston Financial, notes that "The key is to get good people and keep them—otherwise there's no one to delegate to."

Only when a manager delegates does he or she have *time* to do several critical things: develop staff as individuals and as a team, network in the organization and marketplace, develop and apply new skills, and become a futuristic thinker and creator of an inspiring vision. A manager who is an effective delegator is more likely to have a track record of innovation and a high level of employee loyalty. Both have a significant impact on the bottom line. And both show up as *truths* in the calendar every day because they require that you spend your time differently.

Through delegation, then, managers make the essential transition from *doing it* to *getting it done through others.* The time that delegating frees up can be spent looking beyond the immediate work to understand its role in the larger system; identifying how the operation could be more efficient or otherwise improved; coaching and developing team members; communicating with key executives in other departments; and implementing key improvements at the strategic and tactical levels. It also results in the manager spending considerably more time outside the organization in forums where best practices are shared. In short, the ability to delegate enables the manager to shift the *frame of reference* upward and outward, leaving individual details to competent staff, and to focus instead on strategy and systems-wide issues. Delegating is key to your development and your staff's development. By delegating, your staff members become strong, loyal performers who, ultimately, take on their own leadership positions and become part of your network.

A word of caution here: Delegate does not mean abdicate. Sometimes managers who are working to change their micro-managing tendencies go too far the other way, when they should be trying to strike a balance between providing general direction and coaching. Feedback from staff helps guide you in striking the right balance.

Risk-Taking and Innovation

The demonstrated ability to take smart risks and to devise innovative solutions to business challenges is essential, and, therefore, a powerful element of strong product. Risk-taking and innovation are presented together here because they are interwoven.

There is extraordinary demand for leaders who have successful track records of risk taking and innovation. Demonstrating these capabilities, after all, requires courage, a drive to succeed, and the knowledge that things may not work. Emerging leaders often cite fear of damaging their reputations as the single biggest barrier to risk-taking. And yet, it is only risk-taking that leads to the breakthrough thinking that helps businesses innovate and grow. Think about IBM—a classic *blue chip* corporation: large, stable, and predictable. And yet, since 1890, IBM has been a consistently innovative organization, remaining competitive and relevant by taking major risks in anticipation of changes in business and technology.

Paul Hogan is someone who knows a lot about the benefits of taking smart risks. He says, "The whole concept is managing risk, not avoiding it. And that goes for careers as well. There are three high-risk assignments that can help define your career: developing and launching a new product, opening a new sales territory, or working out a serious problem. Those are the jobs that get attention at the top of the house and none are risk-free. If it fails, it's how you react to it—what did you learn, what would you do differently, and did you take responsibility and communicate early—not look for someone to blame."

To be sure, taking smart risks to drive business performance doesn't always work as one would hope. Those who actively manage their brands know that they mitigate their own risk by ensuring they have a broad and favorable reputation, especially with key decision-makers, and work to ensure that this remains true. A base of support is a vital companion to a track record of risk taking and innovation because supporters, also known as *brand builders,* can soften the blow of a failure by helping the organization see it in the broader context of the player's or team's strong track record.

Many people associate risk with taking a bold action, but it can be just as risky to stand still and do nothing. Business as usual—the business practice of operating as one always has, without making adjustments or more significant change to address new problems and opportunities—is a dangerous practice for both the business and service suppliers within it. Ironically, those who gravitate toward the business as usual approach tend to be more risk-averse, and yet pursuing the course of business as usual *actually creates significant risk* for the organization and those in it. A business as usual approach—doing it as it has always been done—aids and abets the Peter Principle. It helps drive the player toward that zone of incompetence by relying on the same overused approaches and methods called upon for many years—using a set of responses that are no longer sufficient or relevant to meet new challenges. A narrow skill set and over-reliance on proven methods are factors that can and do lock players into an unproductive, stagnant space.

The "Strong Second" vs. the "Corporate Spouse"

It may not be immediately obvious to you why being second in command is risky. To many, it seems like a safe position because you're not on the front of the firing lines. But the *way* the role is fulfilled is where the risk lies.

Almost all players in organizations—including leaders at most levels—are also seconds to their bosses. How you fulfill the role of being a second has a significant impact on your perceived present and future value. While it may seem safer to be a corporate spouse (someone who primarily supports a boss), you will actually strengthen your brand and product by becoming a strong second (someone who also leads), instead. As a strong second, you are more likely to take risks and innovate, and, thus, enhance your brand product and overall value exchange.

The following table shows the difference between a strong second, a player who recognizes responsibility to drive business performance *and* make the boss look good, and a corporate spouse, whose primary role is making the boss look good and demonstrating unquestioned loyalty.

Attitude/Behavior	Strong Second	Corporate Spouse
Role Definition	Regards supporting boss as inherently important, but the primary focus is on holding self and others accountable for business performance. Has his/her own independent deliverables.	Defines primary role as supporting boss and making him/her look good. Does not drive a meaningful independent agenda that is discrete from boss' agenda.
Leadership Approach	Steps out and leads overtly. Makes decisions on his/her own. Seeks appropriate independent visibility, leadership roles, and space.	*Supports*, through quiet influence in the service and shadow of the boss.
Agency	Serves when needed as a trusted stand-in, in order to make good decisions *and advance the business agenda, usually consistent with team's shared vision.*	Can stand in/be point person to advance the boss' agenda ('this is how the boss would want it,' or 'this is what the boss said to do').
Communication	Communicates environmental info to boss; however more often communicates own initiatives.	Holds a special 'insider' position—is conduit for communication to and from the boss, especially on political issues. Is 'eyes and ears' for the boss. Often serves as special 'sounding board.'

Attitude/Behavior	Strong Second	Corporate Spouse
Relationship to Team	Key leader, respected for business impact, capability, and influence with boss.	Considered a factor/dynamic to be worked by others as part of managing the boss.
Currency	Results and loyalty.	Loyalty and support.
Following	Follows to a point, but isn't so close as to miss issues on the near horizon. Is loyal, supports boss while there, but goal is to learn, develop, and use that as a springboard to what's next.	Follows by being 100% loyal, making boss successful. Can get caught up in the hero status ascribed to the boss, missing potential issues and obstructions. Intention is to stay with boss through thick and thin, over the long-term.
Self-actualization	By seeing the impact of his/her ideas and efforts in business performance and results. Does this by realizing upwardly mobile goals, having impact, and having that impact ascribed to/credited to him/her.	Via success of the boss, and through the attention, recognition, and gratitude for loyalty expressed by the boss. Impact is ascribed to/credited to boss or boss' business unit.
Future Potential	Is seen as able to take the leader's job.	Is not seen as successor.
Self-determination	Takes control over own career progression and future business impact.	Gives control away to boss.

The distinction between the strong second and corporate spouse is evident in business impact and has major implications for career advancement. The corporate spouse sets himself or herself up to be almost entirely dependent on the success of the boss. Ironically, the blind loyalty of the corporate spouse can be a contributing factor to the boss' stalling out, or failing altogether, if this individual brings a skewed view of reality to the

boss because of their relationship. In corporate life, mal [...]
good is a given, but it is better to do that while ma[...]
degree of independence that fosters open, honest con[...]
more on what's good for the organization than on blind [...]
A final note: where there is a narcissistic leader there is likely also a corporate spouse.

Elaine's Story: Product in Action

To help us understand the components of product, let's look again at Elaine's feedback, this time zeroing in on product attributes and drags of the "Results-Getter" brand.

Brand Element: Product	Brand Attributes	Brand Drags
Functional expertise and focus	Ability to build sales plans and to forecast; strong grasp of P&L and what drives the numbers.	Too narrow in her focus: looks vertically at her unit, not horizontally at the enterprise.
Leadership	Ability to motivate her people and therefore execute the plan.	Has hired a lot of "B" players; hasn't used technology to aggressively drive productivity.
Management	Results-driven; hands-on; gets to the point.	Tendency to micro-manage, spending less time engaging with broader enterprise and senior management.
Risk tolerance and innovation	No noted strengths	Takes the proven route vs. developing new, innovative solutions.

While Elaine toils away each day, she may begin to see others win and/or advance while she stays where she is. This can be a mystery to some players, who perceive themselves as working very hard, often putting in ery long hours, and getting strong results. They ask, "Why am I not getting those same opportunities and/or being rewarded that way?" They see opportunities offered to others who appear (to them) to be less productive when, in fact, these others have evolved to contribute at the next level of value—as enterprise thinkers, strategists, and problem solvers.

In this case, Elaine is operating in an outmoded mindset; her colleagues are not. They are actively building broader alliances and are contributing as business executives first, and functional leaders second. Based on her product feedback, Elaine sits squarely in the center of the continuum shown earlier—in the managerial role. It is not unusual for middle managers like Elaine to learn they need to be more strategic, but they may need help putting this into practice.

Elaine faces hurdles in each of the four product component areas: becoming a strategic thinker and contributor, involving herself in continuous learning, finding new solutions through innovation and/or prudent risk-taking, and attracting and growing top talent. By getting feedback and developing and implementing an action plan, Elaine will be able to reposition herself from Results-Getter to executive/emerging organization leader.

Let's look at how Elaine responded to her product feedback and the actions she took to create a stronger product in her marketplace.

Elaine's Strategic Frame of Reference

Based on her feedback, it's clear that Elaine's core skills as a sales manager center on her numbers orientation and focus on results. Elaine is a classic example of the "Results-Getter" brand. When you examine the attributes column, building and executing sales plans are at the center of her value exchange and have contributed to her development of a successful track record. The drags column, however, adds important texture to this picture of a sales professional at mid-career. Each of her strengths is now beginning to develop a shadow, or downside, indicating an area in need of improvement. Earlier in her career, as Elaine was moving up, it made sense for her to be focused on her division's performance—to focus intensively on achieving results. This focus and discipline helped her exceed her sales goals year after year. She has now, however, reached a level in her organization where her marketplace needs different things from her. She is now expected to act more like an executive: to run her part of the business while looking beyond it at the larger organization, and to think conceptually; to see patterns, make connections, and seize opportunities that exist across functions, markets, and global territories; to empower her team to deliver the results while she turns her attention upward and outward, across business units, and the enterprise, in order to anticipate next opportunities and work in new ways to seize them. This includes collaborating in new ways with an ever-expanding set of business partners.

Elaine's product data, however, indicate that she is still spending most of her time in the details of the business (micromanaging with a vertical focus). Her peers, meanwhile, are delegating the details to others. This inability to delegate is a key reason that she has failed to attract "A" players. "A" players tend to value autonomy and the freedom to run with their own ideas. Developmentally, Elaine is now a prisoner of the cycle her Results-Getter brand has created: working the details, micromanaging, and attracting and retaining the "B" players who are more comfortable being told what to do and how to do it. It is a self-fulfilling cycle that can only change if she changes how she approaches her work.

Elaine decided that she needed help in shifting her strategic frame of reference. As mentioned, she began working with a professional coach; by allowing herself to be open to what she might learn, Elaine positioned herself for important professional growth. Her first important step—obtaining market feedback through her coach—helped her understand the degree to which her self-definition aligned with that of her marketplace.

Her first impulse was to respond in a transactional way to her feedback: "OK, I just need to stop micromanaging," and "I need to hire 'A' players next time." But as she continued to think about her approach to work, she realized that she needed to make more fundamental changes—involving both persona and product—in order to progress and bring true value to her organization. In essence, her Results-Getter brand was derailing her ride to the top. Her no-nonsense, task-driven, 'just get to the point' manner was viewed as singularly focused on her sales results at the expense of an expanded frame of reference that included the broader issues of importance to the entire enterprise.

Over the next twenty-four months, Elaine began a purposeful, deliberate effort to expand her strategic frame of reference and to reposition herself as an executive-level service supplier, with broader organizational focus and increased patience.

Elaine's Continuous Learning

To help achieve this repositioning, Elaine wisely identified a business opportunity that could serve as the focal point of her efforts to deliver value in a new way. She began attending industry forums and roundtables where best practices were presented by leading research firms and think tanks. In the past, she had tossed invitations to these events into the trash, thinking they were a distraction that would slow her down from achieving sales results. On the rare occasions when she did attend, she was apt to be out in the hallway on her cell phone dealing with staff and customer issues most of the day, not actually participating in the sessions. At one of these forums, a new knowledge management advancement caught her attention, and upon conducting further research, she determined that it could benefit her division *and* many other customer divisions in her organization as well. The discovery of this opportunity made her a new believer in the value of continuous learning at the same time that it offered her a chance to innovate by taking a prudent risk.

Elaine's Risk-Taking and Innovation

After the forum, Elaine created a proposal recommending that the new knowledge management practice be introduced at her company. It would require a sizable investment and focused cross-functional leadership over two years to complete the initial launch. She also proposed that she lead this effort, while retaining management oversight of her team.

"I recognized I was taking risk—both for the business because of the size of the investment in dollars and people, and for me, because if I failed, it would be pretty public," Elaine recalled. She presented her ideas first to her boss, who was supportive of the concept but preferred to pass it off to a staff function for continued development. Her boss wanted to ensure Elaine's focus would remain on revenue generation. Elaine recognized through this transaction that her relationship with her boss was enabling her own undesirable results-getter tendencies. She realized she needed to gain her boss' support in her repositioning efforts, and that the contract between them, in terms of expectations of her role, needed to change. She ultimately convinced her boss to support her goals, which included restructuring her team (which she would continue to lead) by elevating a strong performer into a senior role and delegating key aspects of her responsibilities to several members of her group. Not surprisingly, she received no resistance from her team members, who saw the new responsibilities as a sign of their own advancement and potentially greater visibility.

Elaine began meeting with key players to discuss her idea informally and generate both critique and support of it. In developing relationships with players in these areas, she was very conscious of the need to work harder at establishing personal rapport, building relationships first, and getting to the work second. Some of the meetings happened over lunch or dinner. One meeting took place at the golf course. She took time to get to know her colleagues, seeing this richer kind of connecting as a key aspect of her actual work—not as a discretionary activity to be pursued only if she had time and/or happened to like the colleague. These relationships would serve her well during difficult times in the months to come.

Elaine received approval to lead the project, and she and her team presented monthly progress updates to the executive committee. Elaine said, "I saw it as a great opportunity to get in front of the leadership of the company, and create an impression that I was a big picture thinker, who could also implement a sophisticated strategy. At first, I was concerned that I was leaving the legitimate side of the business—my line duties—for a soft project. The more we discussed it, though, I realized this was an extraordinary opportunity to learn holistically about how the business worked, and to have a major impact on how we fundamentally relate to and serve our customers."

Within a matter of weeks, Elaine found herself spending her time radically differently than she had in her sales manager role. She immersed herself in information on knowledge management from a wide range of sources, including industry think tanks, consulting firms, a university, and other professionals in the new and rapidly expanding network she was developing. Each new piece of information reshaped and refined her vision for her initiative. In effect, she had raised her sights upward and outward—across functional units and teams in her organization, outwardly to the rich external resources and network she had begun to build. Because she needed to develop a new capability that would fit not her organization as it existed today, but as it would two years down the road—she also become a futurist of sorts—seeing the world as it would be, not as it was. In effect, she developed the capacity to think like the CEO. In two years' time, Elaine and her team achieved the initial launch of a powerful global knowledge management system that reshaped the way wholesale business was conducted at her organization.

After the launch, Elaine found herself in a quandary. "I had grown tremendously through the project, and my staff really rose to a new level of contribution too. I knew as the project was starting to wrap up that I did not want to go back to my sales management role, and I really couldn't have. There were others who were doing it quite well and it would have demoralized people to have me return. I knew I was taking this risk when I initiated the whole idea two years earlier, and it didn't seem right to ask for a promised assignment at that time."

So Elaine initiated conversations about what she might do next within her organization. One of these was with the CEO, now a mentor and fan of hers, but with whom she had only infrequent contact until her work on the initiative began. Over a series of subsequent discussions in which Elaine shared her vision and point of view on organizational threats and opportunities, the CEO and Elaine identified a role leading a series of wholesale businesses. This position placed Elaine on track to join the senior management team in several years. "I don't think I ever would have had the opportunity to run multiple business units if I hadn't lead the knowledge management initiative," she said. "And I shouldn't have. In retrospect, I was doing my job as a results-getter long after I should hav evolved into a senior player. If I hadn't taken the special assignment, I would not have had the opportunity to see across the whole enterprise, to gain the extremely valuable views and insights of a lot of talented people in this company, and to let go of a way of thinking and *doing*—that was making me stale. I had to get out of it to see it."

Elaine's Delegation Skills and Ability to Grow Talent

As part of managing their own advancement, professionals in the early to middle stages of their careers are intensively focused on delivering results. Developing this kind of track record is their best assurance that they will continue to get promoted and recognized for their efforts.

But by mid-career, most service suppliers are called upon to demonstrate the capacity to shift from being a hands-on results-getter with a vertical focus to a leader and coach who can teach and empower others to do this work. This enables the service supplier to contribute value by interfacing with the organization on cross-functional and enterprise-wide strategic concerns, providing thought leadership, synthesis of inter-business unit issues, and a well-developed point of view on the issues and path to pursue.

In a way, Elaine forced herself to make this transition when she took the risky step of pursuing a leadership position on a new business initiative. She no longer had time to micromanage her staff, which in turn forced her to delegate to emerging stars on her staff. She discovered, to her surprise, that they were more than ready to accept the challenge, which in turn made Elaine function as someone who had an eye for hiring and developing talent.

Development Plan

	e's Brand: line	Development Tactics	Elaine's Brand After Leading the Knowledge Management Initiative
Persona	Results-getter extraordinaire	Reached out to develop peer relationships well beyond her silo, and consciously spent time establishing rapport, creating connections, and only then moving to the work.	Strategic contributor ready to step into next-level P&L assignment with solutions and optimism
Persona	Singular focus on results	Negotiated an evolved relationship and expectations with her boss. Committed to establishing as a priority in all relationships.	Well-rounded emerging executive with solid social skills.
Product	Driving her own numbers	Attended industry forums and paid attention at them; introduced and drove Knowledge Management initiative at her organization. Linked in think tanks, consultants, academics, and others to shape her thinking.	Seeing across the enterprise; able to synthesize complexity and boil it down to the one or two critical elements

Brand Dimension	Elaine's Brand: Baseline	Development Tactics	Elaine's Brand After Leading the Knowledge Management Initiative
Product	More of a tactician	Restructured her team, leaving tactics to others while she focused only on strategy.	Tactician and strategist.

Persona and Product: The Center of Your Value Exchange

In Chapters 2 and 3, we have explored persona (the emotive, emotional connection and reaction you elicit in others as a result of your personal energy, attitude, style, vision and values) and product (the skills, capabilities, expertise, and track record of results that you bring to your work). Persona and product are two key essential inputs to the creation of a powerful and differentiated exchange of value between you and your market. Your unique strengths and passions, managed correctly and coupled with a commitment to integrity and enthusiastic participation, will make you a supplier of choice—a leader of choice—in your marketplace. What are the specific dimensions of your brand that positively differentiate you, in terms of persona and product? When combined, what is the basis of your brand value? How does that value translate into bottom-line business performance? Your ability to answer these vitally important questions with powerful answers is the key to having and managing a strong brand. Again, because brands exist in the context of a given marketplace, your challenge is to ensure that your market's experience of you and your value is as strong as you intend it to be.

Having worked with thousands of professionals to develop their brands, it is my observation that individuals have a dominant strength—either persona or product—and they lead with that strength. This is evidenced in the feedback they receive on their brands. For example, one leader received this feedback on his brand: "The sheer force of his positive attitude and energy has helped drive this organization forward, in spite of the rest of us." It's a very revealing quote, giving great insight into this leader's persona and how he leverages it to achieve results. Another leader, by contrast, received this feedback: "She is a trusted advisor, sees two years ahead, and brings thought leadership to any conversation." This is a product-based strength. This is important to know because the marketplace is validating aspects of each leader's brand thereby differentiating them. Although one leads with persona and the other with product, their brand management work is the same: Protect and grow what is working especially well, and ensure that the core strength/dominant brand attribute is rounded out with other dimensions of value that complement it. The first leader, for example, must ensure that he is bringing both charisma *and* thought leadership, strategic acumen, and other aspects of product to his market. The second must ensure that she genuinely connects on a personal level with others, and is able to use a sophisticated set of social and interpersonal skills to advance her agenda.

Do you lead with persona or product? Think about this as you fill in your Brand Development Plan Worksheet.

Summary

In this chapter we explored how to grow your product over time to ensure that your value exchange stays strong in the face of evolving market need. Coasting is tantamount to taking yourself out of the game. You either grow and build on your value, while developing good working relationships with co-workers with a broad range of styles, or your brand loses its power and you slide to the margin. Moving from details to big picture, thinking conceptually and across systems, being a strategic player, knowing the difference between managing and leading, and knowing how to engender smart risk-taking and innovation—these are all inherent in strong brands—particularly at mid-career.

Update your Brand Development Plan Worksheet now

As you read this chapter, did you gain a clearer picture of your product? In the section on the four components of product, did you discover that you needed to work on one or more of them in order to have a stronger product? Do you need to take more risks or learn to delegate? Should you be taking on challenging assignments at work to help develop leadership skills? Take a moment now to note the changes you want to make and add them to your Brand Management Plan Worksheet before moving on to packaging in the next chapter.

Chapter 4

Packaging

What Is Packaging?

Packaging is the 'wrap' you place around your product. Since your product is who you are and how you think, your packaging therefore starts with the way you wrap yourself—it begins with personal appearance. It extends to all the ways your ideas manifest themselves at work—written reports and other communication, such as emails. It includes your 'surround'—the quality of the talent you've populated your team with, for example. So as you can see, packaging is a whole lot more than "dress for success."

Packaging is a key driver of brand management. In consumer goods, it's the familiar look of the toothpaste we use, the label in the clothes we wear, the wrapper on the food we eat, the beverages we select. For most of us, packaging is the first way we experience a product (or a person)—through our sense of sight.

Packaging has always been important. The Greeks and Romans and other societies around the world were as concerned about personal packaging as our society is today. For proof, you only have to look in museums at early cosmetics, jewelry, and fine clothing that have been used for adornment for the past 5,000 years. Things haven't changed much, have they?

Some people will argue that packaging shouldn't be important, that we shouldn't judge a book by its cover, or that only the quality of one's ideas should matter. The reality, however, is that others *see* our packaging before they hear our product—our thinking. Packaging paves the way for each of us to be heard and understood in a particular way. It can either get in the way of how our ideas and intellect are appreciated, or it can support our goal to be understood and appreciated for the quality of our thinking. It would be nice if packaging didn't matter, but while it does, make sure yours works for you. Manage your packaging to direct your market's attention to where you want it to be—on the substance of your value exchange and the impact you are having on business outcomes.

To illustrate how packaging affects what people think of you or remember about you, take this short quiz. What comes to mind first when you think of each of the people below?

Dennis Rodman
Bella Abzug
George Hamilton
Minnie Pearl
Don King

Now, can you list each person's achievements? That's more difficult, isn't it?

In the table below, I've supplied some answers you might have generated.

Name	First Recall	Performance/Major Achievements
Dennis Rodman	Flamboyant	Two-time NBA Defensive Player of the Year. Five-time NBA Champion. Led NBA in rebounding for seven consecutive seasons.

Name	First Recall	Performance/Major Achievements
Bella Abzug	Oversized, flashy hats	Co-authored original Freedom of Information Act. Founder of National Women's Political Caucus. Sponsored Title IX, changing the landscape for girls and women in sports.
George Hamilton	Great year-round tan	Fifty-year film and television career as actor and producer. More than 100 film or television appearances including *The Godfather Part III*. Three Golden Globe nominations, one win.
Minnie Pearl	Straw hat with $1.98 price tag	Country Music's preeminent comedian for fifty years. Member of Country Music Hall of Fame.
Don King	Extraordinary hairdo	Promoter of the biggest boxing productions in history and more than 500 world championship fights. Promoted six of the ten largest pay per view events in history. First promoter to create his own television network.

It's interesting, isn't it, that, despite their considerable achievements, these individuals are best remembered for a peculiarity or distinctive aspect of their personal packaging. These are people who have achieved levels of success most of us will not realize in our lifetimes, and yet our first inclination was to think of their packaging, and perhaps even to discount them because of it.

These political and entertainment figures illustrate an important point that can be applied to the business world. CEOs and other business leaders need to pay attention to their packaging to make sure it reinforces the message they are trying to send. It might be possible to find a CEO who has a distinctive aspect of his or her packaging, but it would be the exception, not the norm. While it might be desirable—even essential—to stand out via packaging in the entertainment industry, it's almost always unacceptable in business. Do you think Donald Trump could have gotten away with a comb-over before he became his own boss? And the preoccupation with his hair just proves the point that you don't want your packaging to be so distracting that people can't help but focus on it. A good rule of thumb about packaging is that if it distracts, it detracts.

While the quiz above demonstrates the importance of personal appearance, packaging is about more than just the way you look. It's also about your environment and the people with whom you choose to associate at work. Let's look at the components of packaging.

The Components of Packaging

Your "Wrapping"

It may help us understand the importance of your wrapping (your clothing and appearance) if we liken them to consumer goods packaging, which is created to enhance the product and reinforce the image of the brand. Similarly, your clothing and your appearance speak volumes about your personal brand.

Of course, the packaging of a product helps us identify it quickly and determine what its function is. But the importance of packaging extends well beyond functionality. Packaging is the means by which marketers get customers' attention, and then communicate with and influence them. In a way, this is what your clothing and appearance do for you. And that is why it is so important to make sure the attention you're getting is the kind of attention you want.

Indeed, the success of some consumer products can hinge on the package's ability to attract the buyer and to call attention to the unique characteristics contained within—especially when the product's fundamental characteristics are pretty much like those of their competitors. This is also true for you in comparison to your colleagues in your organization.

Today's consumer goods packaging experts are well versed in human psychology, and we can all learn a lot from them. They know what colors evoke certain kinds of emotions in us; they know that our brain will respond to the word "new" on a label. They know which techniques to use to catch your eye and call attention to their product in a crowded, competitive marketplace. Leaders can use this same psychology to enhance their packaging and make sure it supports their unique personal brand.

What does your appearance say about you? Is your wrapping sending the right message to your market?

Standing Out vs. Fitting In

While you want your packaging to help you stand out from the crowd, you also have to be sure that it helps you fit in with others in your organization. Although this sounds contradictory, it really isn't.

Think about uniforms and how they help identify individuals as members of a larger group. Clergy, healthcare providers, baseball players, soldiers, school children, religious sects, postal carriers, and firefighters wear uniforms to signal their membership, and sometimes their rank, in their organization.

The corporate world has its own version of the uniform. Often there's a company *look* that is the standard, and there's an expectation that organization members will conform to it. Whether it's formal business attire, business casual, a nametag or lapel pin, or some variation, every organization has both stated and subtle rules about personal packaging.

While consumer packaging experts try to make their products *stand out* to catch our eye, packaging in the workplace is all about *fitting in,* not standing out. Often this is difficult for Americans, in particular, because of our keen focus on individuality. But at work, the focus is on demonstrating your membership on the team, not on standing out by the way you look.

The whole point here is to encourage standing out through your powerful exchange of value, not through idiosyncratic aspects of your packaging. Packaging anomalies—even subtle ones such as wrists draped in jewelry that clinks and jangles, outdated ties or wardrobes, ill-fitting clothes—create a call-out to one or more of our five senses and send a signal that the person doesn't fit in. When this is the case, it is just that much harder to get others to see the value of your leadership brand.

Your Environment

Packaging extends beyond your personal appearance to the physical environment you create. At senior manager levels, we might not *talk* all that much about whether a peer's office space is tidy or not, but we *notice* it, don't we? Can you think of someone you work with whose office is piled high with stacks of folders, papers, mementos, or junk? I bet you can. A messy workspace is stressful to look at. And if the person who owns the space also works excessive hours, we really take note. What conclusions might you draw in that case? How would your conclusions affect your impression of that person's brand?

Brand feedback for clients who work long hours in a messy office sounds like this: "I know it shouldn't be a big deal, but I do want to mention that John's workspace is sloppy. It gives the sense that he's not organized, and I am concerned he isn't able to prioritize...it's just the sense I get." Or like this: "She's got piles and piles of stuff in her office; and she's apt to be late...it creates a sense that she's disorganized and won't deliver on the work you need. It makes you question her trustworthiness and dependability. I have to be honest and say I am a little embarrassed by how she keeps her space; it's a bad reflection on our team."

If your desk is a mess and your office is cluttered, clean them up now. Don't wait for other people to say something. Often feedback on this issue, like feedback on clothing, is so subtle that you might overlook it or never receive it at all—and think that this aspect of your packaging isn't negatively affecting your brand. But it is. It's a staller now that will ultimately be a stopper. If you need more proof, just look at the desks of CEOs. They are almost always neat and orderly. Take your cue from them.

Your Team

The leader is understood partly in the context of the company he or she keeps. If you are a manager, your team—from your administrative assistant onward—is part of your packaging.

I have known executives who had administrative assistants with brands bigger than their own: "He's such a nice guy but his admin will cut you at the knees and she's had me in tears. I hate it when I have to deal with her. Why would such a nice guy allow that to go on?" You can bet that the negatives associated with this executive's team member are having a detrimental effect on his packaging. This is why it is so important to assemble a strong team and manage it well. Not doing so means others are responding to the distraction, not the substance.

Take a close look at the team you've got—specifically the talent reporting to you. The quality of the talent on your team says volumes about your standards, capabilities, and self-confidence. How do they reflect on you as a manager and leader? Are they mostly "A" players or mediocre performers? Do they all—or at least the ones closest to you—look, act (and likely think) the same—maybe in fact a lot like you? If your team is mediocre, how can you be stellar? If your team is homogenous, how likely is innovation to occur? Do they represent your business (and you) well as they go about their work? What conclusions will your organization marketplace draw about you based on how your people bring themselves to work, and how they behave and perform?

Make Your Packaging Direct Your Market to Your Value

Ultimately, your packaging affects your ability to create choices for yourself at work, as these three examples show:

- A professional who was promoted to senior vice president at a large multinational organization reflected on her promotion. She recalled a moment years ago that was the turning point in her relationship with her manager. "I joined a new area in the organization, coming from a division where I had been dressing casually to match my customer's dress," she said. "One day my new boss mentioned something in a very quiet, casual aside—I could easily have missed it, he said it so subtly. 'You may be used to casual, but in this group we all wear our jackets.' I started wearing a blazer, and sure enough, people in the group started treating me more seriously. My boss started sharing more feedback and coaching me on how to be more effective. In the end, I think his willingness to tell me about the dress rules, and my demonstrating I heard him, helped align me for promotion to partner. If I hadn't listened, my boss and my group would probably still be stuck on the fact that I wasn't wearing a jacket."

- During a brand management workshop, a female participant received feedback from a colleague that "it might be a good idea to stop wearing your casual, open-toed sandals on casual days." The woman was incensed! Who was this colleague to tell her how to dress for work? As they talked it over, the woman learned that her attire was an issue because her colleague wanted to include her in an industry networking lunch at a high-end restaurant, but was reluctant to do so because the unspoken dress code was formal business attire. The feedback was intended to support the inclusion of this colleague in a beneficial business-networking event, essential to sustaining and building the power of one's value exchange. Because people are sometimes offended by feedback on their personal appearance, others are hesitant to share this potentially valuable information, and people's careers can suffer because of it.

■ Torrance Childs, a financial services executive and African American, recounts a moment when he saw *Fortune* magazine's "Black Power" issue. "At the time, my personal brand was that of 'nice guy,' but I was trying to get people to see me for my results," Torrance noted. "When I looked at the cover of the magazine, I saw black executives who were dressed in crisp suits, who wore contemporary glasses—everything about them said 'professional' and 'I mean business.' I went out the next day and replaced my 'nice guy' teardrop glasses with edgier ones, upgraded my brand of shirts, bought some new suits, and committed to losing forty pounds. I realized that I could manage my packaging to get others to see me the way I see myself and as I want to be seen—as a results-driven business leader with the potential to have even greater impact."

Summary

Packaging is the third of the 5 P's and is an essential part of a strong leadership brand. Packaging is all about fit and focus: showing you are a member of the larger team and focusing your organization marketplace on the true substance of your value exchange. It includes your attire, your written and verbal communication, your office, and your team. Every organization has rules about packaging and yours should direct attention to your value, not detract from it. Packaging should be a strategic consideration as you build your unique value exchange and bring it to market. If packaging issues are distracting your marketplace and directing attention to the wrong place, remove them from your brand mix and redirect attention to your talents and value exchange.

Update your Brand Development Plan Worksheet now

Are there aspects of your packaging that you need to change to reinforce the leadership brand identity you want to create in your marketplace? What are they? Does your attire send the message that you fit into the organization and understand the culture there? Does your office reinforce the impression that you are organized and reliable? How do the members of your team reflect on your brand? If there are steps that you plan to take to enhance your brand via packaging, make a note of them now on your Brand Development Plan Worksheet.

Chapter 5

Promotion

Let's try another quiz to get us started on promotion. Whose name is synonymous with Motown? Did you answer Berry Gordy? When you think of the song, "My Girl," do you think of The Temptations? When you think "Stop, in the Name of Love," do Diana Ross and The Supremes come first to mind for you? If you answered yes to these questions, you missed a name—in fact you missed *the* name that is behind Motown, and hundreds of Motown hits including those mentioned. That name is The Funk Brothers. "The Funk Brothers are the virtuosos of jazz and R&B who put the fire and soul into Motown's greatest hits. But memories of Motown are memories of the Four Tops, Marvin Gaye and Smokey Robinson, while the men who actually built that Detroit groove rarely made the liner notes," according to National Public Radio's Dick Gordon. The Funk Brothers are a stunning example of tremendously talented individuals who worked behind the scenes in the music industry for decades but who did not get credit for their extraordinary achievements.

It's interesting to compare The Funk Brothers with another entertainer: Barry Manilow. Like The Funk Brothers, Manilow is also a great singer and composer with many songs made famous by other performers. The difference is he's well known within the music industry and among the general public for both talents. There's another difference—the well known and well promoted Barry Manilow is a multimillionaire. The relatively obscure Funk Brothers made $10 per song.

What Is Promotion?

Promotion includes advertising, public relations, and marketing communications. The role of promotion is to call attention to a product or service, and build awareness of it, usually with a focus on key benefits, with the ultimate aim of influencing purchasing decisions. Promotion exists both to inform and create awareness, and is an essential aspect of marketing *in competitive markets.*

Each time you see a sign on the wall of a building, you are looking at the oldest known form of advertising. Archaeologists have unearthed an outdoor advertisement from ancient Rome that offered property for rent. Another, painted on a wall in Pompeii, invited travelers to visit a tavern in a nearby town. Town criers were medieval figures, but they were also the original word-of-mouth advertisers. Promotion has been around for thousands of years because it works.

As one of the 5 P's, promotion is, simply stated, your strategy to ensure that your marketplace has answers to these questions: Who needs to know about me, my team, and my work? What do I choose for them to know? How will I share it with them in a way that's useful *to them*?

The power of effective promotion can be measured in at least two important ways: first, in terms of sales; and second, in terms of overall strength of the brand, with a focus on *awareness, and favorable recall.* Think about the last few significant purchases you have made. A car, perhaps, or appliances, or a computer. What did you factor into your purchase decision? In any of these purchases did you go with a brand you'd never heard of, or did you ultimately go with one that you had previous knowledge or awareness of, and that you were positively predisposed toward—either through personal experience or word of mouth from others? My bet is it's unlikely that you made a major leap of faith on a key purchase—one that involved spending a significant sum of money, for something you will rely upon greatly (a computer or car, for example). Instead, you considered things like quality, consistency, reliability, and other concerns specific to the product and your relationship with it. And when it comes to how people in organizations select talent, the decision process follows the same pattern. That is why brand awareness is critical for you and your team.

In organizational life, the senior-most decision-makers—the buyers—are typically straight white men. Many of these decision-makers are actively working to expand their frames of reference when it comes to talent selection because they know they must in order to win. They know businesses that win today have three things: consistently superior talent, a thirst for inclusion, and a climate that thrives on new ideas. They know they need to supplement their own natural networks and awareness of available talent because the best talent may not be the most visible talent, depending on where you're looking. Today's leaders know they only add value to their own brands by demonstrating the capability to find, attract, engage and grow the best talent, and doing so means they must tap into circles well beyond their own.

While the decision-makers—the buyers—work the issue from their end, you can work it from yours, whether you are a senior leader or organization newcomer, by (1) ensuring you have a powerful and differentiated exchange of value (persona and product), and (2) by ensuring you are a name brand by creating levels of awareness of yourself and your value exchange so that you come to mind when key appointments and selections are made. Doing this will give your marketplace a solid context for who you are and what you do that transcends any single event—positive or negative—that might be a data point on your brand. This is true for everyone in organizations today, especially those who are distanced from the core power structure by race, gender, age or other factors.

Why Promotion Is Important

We know now that strong brands enable their corporate owners to command higher prices for their offerings, reduce the cost of new customer acquisition, enhance customer and employee loyalty, and enable organizations to attract the best talent. Similar benefits hold true for *people* with strong brands too.

If your brand at work is strong, it means it's value-intensive *and well known* in your marketplace. It also is a brand that can claim endorsement by influential players in your organization's power structure. That puts you in greater demand, allows you to command a higher salary, and lets you select from a wider array of choices when it comes to next assignments and opportunities. It also means you are freer to innovate, experiment, and take prudent risks because the marketplace will be more forgiving of you, as it was of Johnson and Johnson when the Tylenol crisis hit, and as it was of Coca-Cola when the New Coke launch failed. The opposite is also true. If you are not well known or if people have unfavorable recollections of you, or if you lack sponsorship, you will not *sell* as well as the established brand, and you won't be as forgiven if you make a mistake.

We also know that promotion is essential in competitive work environments, and every work environment today is competitive. This is a hard reality of organization life: It doesn't matter if you are brilliant if you are also invisible, or only modestly visible, or if you have high levels of the wrong kind of awareness. Promotion is a major element in influencing success, and when it comes to your own promotion, you have extraordinary control over it. And yet even the term self-promotion conjures up negative images. "He's a shameless self-promoter." "She takes credit for other people's work." "He's always putting someone else down to make himself look better." "She loves to hear herself talk in meetings." These images reflect assumptions and attitudes some people hold about promotion—that in fact, this is what we mean by promotion, when in truth it is not. These are examples—probably familiar to you—of failed promotion. They are examples of people spotlighting themselves, simply because they need the spotlight to boost their egos or feed personal insecurities. These examples can rile us on a very personal level because they can be offensive, unethical, and call the offending party's personal integrity into question. They offer rich revelations and insights into the person, but add no value to the larger business dialogue.

Earlier in this book we noted that your brand is like a mosaic that exists as an image in the minds of others. This image of you is made up of many impressions from stories told about you, from second-hand exposure to your work (reports you create, for example), and from the personal experience others have of you. While you can't control all of the impressions, you can control many of them by managing your brand through promotion. Remember, strong brands are managed outcomes, and promotion is central to creating the outcomes you desire.

Effective Promotion Begins with Intention

Promotion involves making others aware of your accomplishments, and it is an important and necessary part of achieving your brand goals. It is difficult for some people. This may stem from their upbringing, personality type, culture or any number of factors. For them, promotion conjures up the notion of self-aggrandizement and is offensive. The truth, however, is that for most of us, defining promotion in this way makes it unpalatable and undoable.

But what if you had been taught to think of promotion as a means of informing your colleagues and your manager, appropriately, of the great thing you just did that will help your company save time and money? If you think of promotion as sharing useful information, you might find it easier to do. And you have to get comfortable doing it because your career and your advancement depend on it.

When promotion works, it does not create any kind of value-tension or conflict for you or others. This is because you're clear about what you're doing, why you're doing it, and who needs to benefit from it. When it works, promotion is effectively building awareness of you and your value exchange—the benefits of your brand—in the right ways with the right market segments. As we noted earlier, it answers these questions: Who needs to know about you, your team, and your work? What is it you choose for them to know? Why should they care and what's in it for them? It takes concerted energy and focus to manage promotion, and it is work. But it isn't optional, as the Funk Brothers outcome illustrates. If you don't effectively promote, you will pay the price, and it is usually a significant one.

When promotion is well executed, it benefits many parties. The CEO, for example, learns about something and someone that's working well in the organization, and immediately looks to expand that great thinking and success. The business partner learns of a new way to approach a problem, and to realize a more successful outcome. The manager gets the opportunity to recognize the good efforts of a direct report, which is not only good positioning for the direct, but also reflects well on the manager.

Effective promotion begins with your intention. If you promote with the intent to bring true value to others with whom you communicate your successes, or your innovative or strategic thinking, you will have an easier time getting positive data points—the data points you choose for others to have—into the minds of those in your target market. If your promotion comes from a place of personal insecurity or fear, it will strike a different chord among those in your market, and will build up a negative side of your brand.

What's the cost of not effectively promoting yourself? You miss opportunities (assignments, promotions, higher salaries) that get offered to the better known competitor. As you respond to the missed opportunity by working harder and harder, but still not boosting your visibility and awareness, you get angrier and angrier when you are passed over for the next opportunity and the next one. At some point, you become a person you used to chastise—the person with the chip on his or her shoulder. You become frustrated and cynical—and all of a sudden your marketplace begins dealing with you through your chip—not you. Who owns all of this? You do, if you opted out of taking responsibility to promote your brand. You do, if you dismissed the need to promote as offensive or as something only 'certain kinds of people' do.

Effective vs. Ineffective Promotion

In managing your brand, promotion involves:

- getting your achievements and those of your team on the right radar screens for the right reasons;

■ constantly working to be an active participant in the business discourse through your own unique perspective, ideas, and point of view.

I'm talking about effective promotion. You'll only succeed if you understand how effective promotion differs from ineffective promotion. Ineffective promotion is:

■ using only I, me, or my when describing successes or achievements;

■ taking credit for someone else's work

■ building yourself up by putting someone else down (a phenomenon that is especially prevalent when resources are scarce—during downsizings and mergers, for example, when people feel pitted against each other to keep their jobs);

■ inserting yourself into someone else's 'recognition moment' or visibility opportunity—especially one designed to benefit a staff member vs. the boss;

■ pandering to the boss.

Can you think of examples of each of these in action? They seem so blatantly misguided, so obviously ill advised; yet they go on every day in most organizations.

In addition to ineffective promotion, there is another ill-advised behavior that can sabotage your brand. It's a bit trickier to detect and very difficult to correct because it involves an attitude. The attitude manifests itself in statements like these: "I'll put my nose to the grindstone, I'll do exemplary work, I'll work long and hard, and the rest will take care of itself. I think promoting my brand is beneath me and just plain wrong." If this sounds like you, take note. There is danger and trouble ahead. Here's why: If you do not effectively promote yourself and your accomplishments, you take yourself out of the game. You simply cannot assume that just because you worked really hard and did something great last quarter (or last week) that the people who should know about it do know about it. In fact, it's safer to assume they don't. The truth is that, in the normal course of business, we think considerably more often about ourselves than anyone else does. Furthermore, your boss, your boss's boss, and others are overloaded with a full range of issues and concerns that occupy their time and attention. You have to make your way, appropriately, onto their radar screens, and use that time wisely. Doing it well involves both the content of the promotion, and the methods used.

Promotion Is Often Underutilized by Key Players

In organizations headquartered in the U.S., I frequently see American men effectively promote themselves, but I rarely see American women carry it off with the same impact. As Bennie Wiley notes in her foreword to this book, this is true for people of color as well. Unfortunately, many people of color and women think that if they just work hard, their work will speak for itself. In the office, in brief encounters in the hallway, or on the elevator, members of the white male power structure (and the levels below it) talk business and position themselves to be seen as integral to the big picture. Their conversations are about strategy, results, impact, and comparisons to others. This is the direct result of their socialization, it's a well-developed skill, and they have simply carried it forward into work life. The result is that the ability to self-promote in the way that those in power promote is fundamental to personal and leadership brand management. The talk is all about the business and their performance. White men effectively use those brief hallway and elevator encounters as efficient moments of self-promotion by keeping others current on their news and achievements. When you run into a senior colleague once every two or three weeks at the coffee machine, do you talk about the big customer win your team just had or about how the kids are doing? Your shoes? New hairstyle? The topic you raise is a conscious choice, and it has implications for your brand.

Carol Hymowitz, a reporter for the *Wall Street Journal*, has linked the paucity of women in CEO positions to their inability to promote. "Good girls don't advertise. Researchers and female executives cite a variety of reasons for this meager showing: male executives' reluctance to mentor women, women's exclusion from informal networks, a hesitancy to consider women for the toughest posts, and women's own struggle to balance careers and families—sometimes leading them to settle for less-demanding roles at work. But a big factor holding women back is their good-girl, or good-student, behavior."

Some of the leaders I coach—men and women—have noted that men socialized in the U.S. have an easier time accepting praise than do women. Several men have told me that they picked up this important skill well before they reached professional life. Men get comfortable giving and receiving praise and criticism in public as soon as they play on their first sports team. Increasing numbers of young girls are now having this experience, but I think the climate among girls' sports teams—particularly at younger ages—is still less critical and more focused on praise than the average boys' team. My point is not that one is better than the other; rather, that the different emphasis produces different kinds of people. And since most CEOs are men, their rules are the ones we play by.

Why does your ability to accept praise matter in organizational life? Because it signals to others your sense of self-worth. If you receive praise with casual confidence and graciousness, you are communicating to others that you deserve the praise, that your accomplishments make you worthy of a place on the team, and that you are an integral contributor to the success of the business. On the other hand, if you protest too much, you diminish the praise, effectively communicating that you're less worthy and less competent than those around you, and you take yourself off that playing field. Ironically, if you protest, saying you don't deserve the praise, you may appear disingenuous, which can come across as merely a different form of pandering. So, the best way to manage praise as part of effective promotion is to acknowledge it—say "thank you"—and leave it at that.

How to Make Promotion Work for You

What does promotion look like when it works? It's all about your business—the results you achieve and their impact on customers, the P&L, the strategic issues facing the enterprise, the achievements of individuals on your team, and the team itself. To effectively promote your accomplishments, you've got to be thinking about them every day. You have to be on the lookout for ways to recognize the achievements of others, to proactively reach out to colleagues near and far to share good ideas, intelligence, customer insights, and appreciation. As you do this, you create value for them, and it becomes worthwhile for them to listen to you. If you make someone else's job easier by providing better ideas, useful feedback, or advice, what's that person's impression of you going to be? That you're a smart person making important contributions to the business. That you're essential to his or her success. Thus, the brand data points you've created in his or her mind include these attributes: smart, insightful, team player, gets results. You create this impression by knowing what you want your brand to be and then deciding what actions to take to reinforce that impression. You do this through conversations and sharing information that benefits others. When it's put that way, it doesn't sound like self-aggrandizement, does it? Instead, it sounds as it is: helpful and powerful and positive—traits you want associated with your brand. This kind of promotion results only in win-win situations.

Three Promotion Methods

Now that we know promotion is all about focusing on the business, calling attention to wins in a way that's valuable to others, providing useful information, and recognizing others, we can turn to three proven promotion strategies to help you and your brand get recognized for the value you bring. These strategies are called organic promotion, systemic promotion, and brand builder promotion. Let's look at how to use each one.

Organic Promotion Method: the Personal Experience of You

Organic promotion occurs every time you connect with someone—in person or on the phone. Remember, strong brands are managed outcomes and personal experience drives perception. Each day, you have dozens of opportunities to promote in small, subtle ways. These impressions add up (like tiles forming a picture in a mosaic), ultimately accounting for a significant portion of your overall brand identity. An example of organic promotion, then, is your response to a question asked of you many times each day: "How's it going?" If your mission is to build your brand, you'll answer that question with an enthusiastic, high-energy response, referencing your business or some aspect of it. You will squander the opportunity if you offer a benign response such as "Pretty good, thanks, and you?" and move on without waiting for a response, indicating that you really don't care how the other person is. Even worse, you may actually damage your brand by replying with a dour face, failing to crack a smile, rolling your eyes, or answering with "I've been better" or "I'm surviving." The same is true for those reporting to you. And their response, like their brand in general, reflects on them and on you.

The benign response is unmemorable—an opportunity wasted, a mediocrity reinforced. The dour face and sarcastic reply create negative brand data points. The CEO would never reply this way because it would sabotage his or her efforts to keep employees upbeat and productive. So why would you respond this way? The enthusiastic response, on the other hand, helps you build a stronger brand that says you are engaging, energized, upbeat, and substantive. In effect, you reinforce the key qualities of your persona and product—the essence of your value exchange.

I've had clients voice skepticism about this approach, saying that when people ask how you're doing, they don't really mean it. Or they say that a high-energy reply can sound a little over the top and that it's not their style. In the discussion that ensues, the ultimate conclusion is that people want to be around other people—especially other leaders—who are successful, who have some energy, who are meeting their challenges with optimism and making progress. People are attracted to these brand qualities; they are a big part of what makes leaders followable.

Like other aspects of promotion, this can be a stretch for some people, but these are just the people who need to do it. If you find yourself wanting to dismiss promotion as unnecessary or unpleasant, it suggests that this process takes you out of your comfort zone and into your stretch zone. The stretch zone is where you learn and grow, so the best thing you can do is try it, work on it, and evaluate the impact of your efforts on your brand.

Systemic Promotion Method: Tapping into Your Marketplace's Communication Channels

Systemic promotion refers to taking advantage of the formal and informal communication channels, or media, in your organization and using them to get your story out. Examples include internal networks, affinity groups, resource groups, learning circles, lunch groups, newsletters, intranets, web casts, and all the casual connections through which information is exchanged at work. Are you a player in any of these? Could you form a group and play a leadership role in it? Perhaps a monthly brown bag lunch or roundtable with business partners where the purpose is to share knowledge?

A second manifestation of systemic promotion occurs when existing communications are leveraged beyond a single incident. Crisp quarterly reports are a staple of good promotion and should include bulleted highlights of your (or your team's) key accomplishments during the quarter, and their impact on the business. How did each accomplishment improve the business, even if indirectly? Did it make money? Save money? Increase retention? Reduce risk? Taking that second step, translating the feature (the accomplishment) into the benefit (business improvement) is very important. If you don't tell your story, you're giving up power, expecting others to assign some measure of value to you and your work in the organization. Abdicating responsibility for quantifying your impact can result in your being perceived as less valuable, and that's risky for your brand and your career. If you don't take responsibility for doing the work—and it is work—of relating your efforts to the business' performance and improvement, how can you expect others to?

Communicating Your Leadership Brand ROI

The concept of ROI as it relates to leadership brand was introduced in Chapter 1. We learned how to calculate brand ROI in order to gain clarity about our value exchange. Knowing your brand's ROI allows you to succinctly articulate your value exchange and to answer these three questions:

1. How do I describe in jargon-free, benefits-oriented language what I do?

2. What have been highlights of my/my team's/my business' accomplishments in the last twelve months?

3. How much revenue growth, expense reduction, or other business performance improvement did these highlights add up to?

Here's an example (seen through a brief introduction of one person to another in a casual conversation) of how the impact of what you communicate sounds completely different depending on whether you did the hard work of translating your activity into impact:

Example 1 (no translation to impact): "I'm an operations manager."

Example 2 (translation into impact): "I manage operations for two-thirds of the organization. Our team focuses on driving continuous improvement and innovation into core operating practices. Last year we netted a savings of $20 million in operating expense through this approach."

The second example is considerably more powerful. It gets the listener's attention, and creates a powerful impression of value added. The first depicts just another operations manager. In order to make the second example work, the *how* is just as important as the *what*. By this, I mean delivery matters. If it's shared in an egotistical, arrogant tone, it's a potential turn-off. If it's shared in a casual, confident tone, it's going to work and lead to a bigger conversation, and a stronger and more memorable connection. It can only happen for you if you've done the work of clarifying your own exchange of value, including the economic impact associated with it. It is quite powerful when it is done well. Return to Chapter 1 now if you need a refresher on how to calculate your brand's ROI.

If you have difficulty answering the three questions above, you are not alone. Sales professionals have the least trouble because they often think in these terms in their daily work. But many others, including those in staff roles, find it more difficult. But it's a worthwhile exercise because it helps you, and others, see your value to the organization. You might want to make it one of your goals to capture this information on all your future projects. If you need motivation to do it, just remember that there's an external consulting firm for virtually every service provided, including the service you provide, and they'd love to have your work. The consulting firm has figured out how to talk about the economic impact of its work as part of the sales process because it helps them get new business. In other words, it helps them achieve their goals. This same logic applies to your situation. When you think of promotion this way, it's hard to argue against it.

Brand Builder Promotion Method: Who Will Promote You?

Brand builders are influential players in the organization who are major advocates for you and your work. They are your biggest fans. They build your brand in all kinds of places—most importantly in the informal circles of power in your organization where you may not yet be a player.

Brand builders can also represent you in places you can't be—succession-planning discussions, for example, or reorganizations, or selection meetings during mergers and acquisitions. How do you acquire brand builders? You don't. You create them. Brand builders are people who, based on their personal experience of you, and the powerful impression you create about who you are and what you do, are inspired to promote you. They want to 'bring you along' and see you succeed because they believe in you and in your contributions and potential. Ideally, your brand builders include your sponsors, your mentors, your boss, and your boss's boss. If you lead a team, your brand builders should include your team members, especially the top talent. Brand builders should also include key colleagues and, ideally, a diverse base of senior players and rising stars.

A broad base of alliances, including powerful and influential players, is absolutely essential. In turbulent times, some businesses reorganize so frequently that employees no longer even bother reading the reorganization memos since they are out of date minutes after they're printed. One client told me, "There's one a month; I'm tired of it. It's just a distraction at this point." Distraction, maybe, but anticipating power shifts and preparing for them are essential to your own power and longevity. If you don't stay on top of power shifts, you might arrive at work one day to find that your strongest connections are with executives who have been moved to the margin or who have left the organization. Has this happened to you already? If you are a woman or person of color, it's essential to pay attention to this because it's a contributing factor to the access gap. Do the new players know you? Your work? Or do they know you merely as someone associated with a previous power base? Because women and people of color often begin as outsiders to the core power structure, they must rely on others in power to bring them into those circles. Brand builders, then, are especially important for their success.

The Brand Builder Inventory

The key to having a powerful set of brand builders, and a broad base of strong alliances, is to work on it constantly. Think of it the same way you think about starting a new position at a new company. One of the things on your sixty-day plan would be the cultivation of key relationships. Since those in power—officially and implicitly—are changing on an ongoing basis, your sixty-day plan will become an 'every-day' plan with no end date.

The Brand Builder Inventory below will help you create a snapshot of your brand builders. If you have trouble identifying brand builders, think about why that might be, and ask a trusted colleague for some feedback and suggestions on how to start creating some brand builders. There are two important guidelines:

- List only those who are currently active brand builders, not those you hope will become brand builders.

- Do the politically incorrect thing and note each brand builder's relative level of power and influence vis-à-vis the organization's power structure at present.

Brand Builder Inventory

Brand builder (Name)	High Influence	Medium Influence	Low Influence

What does your list show you? How broad or concentrated is your list? Who's on it that you're pleased about? Who's not on it but should be? How diverse is your base of support in your organization? How powerful is this base? The diversity of your brand builder group is an indicator of the degree to which you reach out beyond your comfort zone—beyond your own natural social circles—to create relationships and effectively promote yourself.

The overall strength of this inventory is a function of two things:

■ the degree to which you have created a powerful exchange of value (persona and product) and have effectively focused others on that value exchange

■ the extent to which, through promotion, you have shared it. If you don't like what you see on your brand builder inventory, first ask whether you've got a powerful value exchange. If not, start the difficult but important work of creating one referencing back to chapters 2 and 3. Once you've got a powerful exchange of value, think about your typical communication patterns at work. Who are you getting the word out to? How aggressively? How often? When was the last time you did so? What was the result? What does this tell you about what you need to do next?

What about the Brand Busters in Your Workplace?

This discussion of how you manage promotion has focused on the proactive and the positive aspects of managing your brand. But what about the other side of the conversation—the one that deals with brand busters—those whose mission seems to be to tear you down whenever they have the opportunity? Brand busters are an important market dynamic for many and deserve some attention here.

Consider the case of Jason, a middle manager at a Fortune 500 organization. Jason is a well regarded up-and-comer at his company, known for his strong self-confidence, strategic mindset, and a ten-year track record of opportunistically growing products and businesses under his watch. For the past few years, Jason has been dogged by Corrine, a peer who reports to the same senior vice president. Corrine has grown increasingly brazen in her take-downs of Jason, particularly when he's not present. Colleagues encourage Jason to shake off Corrine's barbs, and yet Jason isn't convinced that it's that simple. After all, Corrine has a very strong relationship with their boss, and her own following is growing. Jason's analysis is that Corrine wants to position herself as heir apparent to the senior vice president, and her one up/one down approach is designed to elevate her at Jason's expense. "I am not sure how to handle this," Jason notes. "If I go after her directly, I could lose because people may hold the aggressive behavior against me. There seems to be a double standard at work—she appears to get away with this stuff but I don't think I could. And yet, doing nothing isn't helping things—she's getting more and more negative, and I think it's hurting me."

Jason's Four Options

Jason has four choices to select from in dealing with Corrine:

Option 1: Do Nothing

Jason is right. If he does nothing, he may find that Corrine's efforts to sour his reputation have some impact with key players. He may also be perceived as weak for not addressing the issue.

Option 2: Take Her on Directly

Jason could simply reach out directly and tell Corrine to back off, or face the consequences of an elevated battle where he responds by working to neutralize or remove her from the playing field.

Option 3: Circle the Wagons

Because Jason has a strong brand and a fairly broad base of alliances, he could work with these individuals to create a circle of resistance around Corrine. He could rally enough support from other key players to force her to back down, as his allies circle around her (by verbalizing and otherwise demonstrating their support for him), as though preparing for battle.

Option 4: Go Elsewhere

Jason could opt out—perhaps because confrontation is 'not his thing,' and take himself and his value to another business unit in his company or to another organization altogether. However, doing so would lend support to Corrine's claims and potentially enhance her stature while detracting from his.

Jason's Course of Action

"I knew I had worked way too hard to allow her to push me out," he recalled. "And I also learned she was burning bridges with others because of her behavior. Ultimately, I decided to meet with her to put it all on the table, tell her I wasn't going to let it go anymore, and insist she stop it. That morning, before we met, she tossed out a critical comment about my P&L in a very public forum, and instead of letting it go, I took her on, right then and there, and she ended up embarrassing herself because she couldn't back up her claim. A colleague correctly read the situation, and jumped in at the end to take her down one more peg. By the time we met one-on-one, she already had a sense of what it would be like if she kept it up with me, and she was clearly feeling less arrogant and more vulnerable. She pretty much backed off after that, although I think her own insecurities made that behavior almost second nature, so there were a few more times that I had to remind her to stop the negative behaviors. I knew that public forums were the most efficient and effective way, so I began to use them. I would not have been comfortable responding in this way if I hadn't first approached her directly and privately to say, 'Stop'. I considered it a shot across the bow, but after that she had to take responsibility for what she said and did. I am glad I stayed the course because we had a change in senior leadership and she is no longer with the company."

Jason borrowed from Options 2 and 3, and built a tactical response that fit within the operating norms of his organization. His sense of permission, which we turn to in the next chapter, was a vital aspect of the foundation from which he confronted Corrine; it was a determinant in his decision not to leave but to push back and claim his own space. All too often, I have seen solid contributors who are conflict-averse or who lack confidence choose what appears to be the easy route—leaving the organization. In the end, this is unfortunate for the individual, who walks away from a large amount of brand equity he or she (and more often it is she) has built in the organization. The organization suffers too, as it loses key talent.

A Promotion Tool: Reach and Frequency

The 'Reach and Frequency' chart is a tool to help you increase awareness of your leadership brand in your organization. It can support your ability to bring rigor and discipline into your efforts to make your brand more visible. This is a tool that advertisers use to quantify the impact of media spending on awareness campaigns. The idea is to define the media plan's impact via (1) the target market segment it is going to reach, and (2) the number of times it will reach those in the segment. I have adapted this tool for use with leaders and emerging leaders because communication and awareness are so essential to engaging and aligning members of the organization around the shared mission. It is also a powerful brand management most people think about themselves considerably more than ....s do, the reach and frequency tool reminds them to reach out and have frequent contact with the key players in their social system. By mid-career, the quality of your relationships, and the people you have them with, are either the limiting factor or the driving force behind what happens next. That is why the 5 P's of Leadership Brand® begin with persona, and include promotion.

A reach and frequency plan can serve as both a plan and a management tool for brand awareness. Here is the template for this plan.

Reach and Frequency Plan to Manage Brand Awareness

Person or team I need to connect with	Objective for connecting	Method(s) I will use	Value I can bring to the person	How often in twelve months will I work to connect	Status (last/next) and notes

Reach and frequency plans are particularly effective for those who need to expand their circle of awareness and influence, and for those in leadership roles who must stay connected with key constituencies. This is a proven tool that without exception produces new opportunities for those who use it. It is especially useful for women and people of color who want to close the access gap—the distance they may experience between themselves and the organization's core power structure.

Summary

Promotion, the actions you take to ensure that your achievements are on the radar screens of the right people in your organization marketplace, is simply essential to a strong brand. Hard work, intelligence, loyalty, and a winning personality are not enough. Being 'invisible' is costly, but self-aggrandizement won't help your career either.

Your leadership brand exists as a series of data points in the minds of others. You have the power and the responsibility to put the right data points out there, in the right ways, to the right market segments, on a regular basis. Why let others define your brand for you when, by practicing the form of promotion described in this chapter with its great emphasis on providing valuable information to others, you can strengthen your market position and increase the likelihood of success, and greater opportunity, for you and your team?

Use these reminders to help you successfully use promotion on a regular basis:

- Find a personal style of sharing information that is comfortable for you.

- Recognize that routine casual encounters are promotion opportunities and use them accordingly.

- Move past personal barriers that prevent you from actively participating in the business discourse—get onto the field and play.

- Adopt a disciplined approach to awareness management: reach and frequency, quarterly reports on your business' performance, knowledge sharing sessions, updating your brand builders with new achievements, and requesting and obtaining placement on visible projects.

- Check your intentions—what are you promoting, why, and who benefits?

- Cultivate your brand builders, and deal with your brand busters immediately.

■ Track your activities and hold yourself accountable to outcomes: employee loyalty among your staff, your ability to attract ambitious players, your own sense of your awareness levels in your marketplace, invitations you receive to join formal and informal groups and teams working on high-impact business challenges.

Update your Brand Development Plan Worksheet now

Now that you've filled in your brand builder inventory, attach it to your Brand Development Plan Worksheet. And while you're at it, fill in the part that addresses promotion. What are you doing to promote your brand? Are you getting your achievements on the right radar screens? Jot down three or four things you can do immediately to begin to promote your achievements and your brand. Identify ways you can use the Reach and Frequency Tool.

Chapter 6

Permission

What Is Permission?

Permission involves believing that you are just as good, if not better, than everyone else around the table, that you have just as much, if not more, to offer, and that you are fully entitled to play on the same field. Others may, and probably do, believe in you, and that is very important. But what's *most* important is that you believe in yourself—that you give yourself permission to feel worthy of access and success. Of course, you also have to be able to deliver on your promises, and hold yourself accountable for outcomes. In any powerful value exchange, a successful outcome is as much about you having impact as it is about you claiming your own place at the table.

Permission Is a Function of Clarity and Confidence

Through your choices, you can control the degree to which the exchange of value between you and your organization marketplace is a robust, *and mutual*, exchange. Taking pride in who you are and in the value you provide, and sharing news about your value (your accomplishments and successes) are some of the choices you can make to begin building the foundation of a strong brand. And they are all components of permission.

An interesting example of permission came from a leadership development seminar I taught at The Partnership, a Boston-based organization whose mission is to help people of color grow and advance. I asked attendees who they thought should be on their brand builder inventory. I expected to get the usual answers: your boss, your boss's boss, your subordinates. But this time I heard something different: The first name on your brand builder inventory should be *your own*. And that is absolutely right. Being your own best brand builder means believing in yourself and trusting yourself to make good decisions and ethical choices, to rebound from your mistakes and failures, and to hold yourself accountable for aiming high and working with rigor and discipline to achieve your goals. After all, if you don't do these things, then why would anyone else? If you are not motivated to pursue being extraordinary, why would others take up your cause?

When it comes to permission, every individual has his or her own starting place. Some people speak of their continuous effort to ward off the forces of self-doubt, and of the emotional energy and attention that this effort takes. For others, it comes more easily, although the autobiographies of even the greatest leaders reveal that they too have moments of self-doubt or questioning. The fundamental difference is that those who afford themselves true permission to engage, participate, and deliver their best effort and result are those most likely to achieve it.

Members vs. Guests: A Useful Way to Think about Permission

Think about the last time you were at a social or business event where both members and guests were present. In member-guest affairs, it's reasonably easy to distinguish between the members and the guests. The members know their way around and comport themselves with the ease and confidence that comes from being comfortable in familiar surroundings. Members belong. Members are legitimate. Members continuously strengthen their bonds with other members. Members help guests navigate through the space, reinforcing their status as 'in the club.' Guests are granted their inclusion only through the good will of the members. Guests are dependent on the members for an invitation to the event, access to resources and services while there, and are able to do only that which members allow them to do. In that sense, guests subordinate themselves to members. This distinction between members and guests exists in organizations, too. Some players in organizations self-select out of membership and instead reclassify themselves as guests. They subordinate themselves to others—to players whom they regard as members—and in so doing, take themselves out of the game.

So how do you think about yourself in your organization? Are you a member or a guest?

Because strong brands are managed outcomes, you have a tremendous amount of control over how you are experienced and perceived by others. As we've seen in the previous chapters on persona, product, packaging, and promotion, brand management begins with the first of three key inputs: your persona. Your persona is your own vision and values, attitude, energy and beliefs, and how you bring those into your environment and through them relate to others. Alongside persona is the second key input to your value exchange: product, or your skills and intellect. Next is how you package this value, and finally how you promote your abilities to your target audience. But here's the hard truth: none of this matters if you don't believe in yourself, or if you lack confidence in your abilities. And that's where permission comes in. If you are waiting for someone else to tell you that you can play on the team, or that your ideas are as legitimate and important as those of everyone else, or that you are as good as the other players in your organization, you will be waiting a long time. The truth is, there is only one person who can give you permission to be a member rather than a guest, and that person is you. Permission is a key input that has direct and profound impact on the relative power of your value exchange.

This sense of legitimacy is one of the foundations of our model—it is your attitude toward yourself that enables you to envision, pursue, and achieve breakthrough results throughout your career. If you are comfortable as a member, are you doing all you can to ensure that others on your team feel this sense of legitimacy too?

Self-Doubt Inhibits Permission

In examining permission, it is important to recognize the higher hurdles those outside of an organization's core power structure must overcome in order to have major impact and career success. We discussed this in the previous chapter on promotion, and it bears repeating here. Some men and women, including those of color, find themselves spending considerable energy tuning in to their internal dialogue of self-questioning. This questioning is often about 'how I should be' in my organization, especially if I am not part of the core power structure. In meetings, for example, these individuals find their focus diverted from the external discussion to their own internal radio station that poses questions such as "How will this person react if I say x, y or z? Should I say it? Maybe I shouldn't." Or "Will they accept what I have to say? Is it acceptable for me to say that? Should I really ask that question or make that point? What if no one agrees, or backs me up?" As the internal questioning continues, the moment in the meeting passes, and the opportunity is lost. Or, this person may acquiesce to this internal radio station for the longer term, and pull back altogether.

The risk is that the voice of the internal radio plays louder, and the voice of the individual—the talented service supplier with unique ideas to contribute—is then not heard in the room. The more distant you are from the organization's core power structure, the more likely this self-questioning will be an issue, detracting from your ability to maximize your impact. In effect, you are at greater risk to relate to the organization as a guest. This member versus guest attitude correlates directly to the relationship of the individual to the core power structure. If people see themselves as outsiders based on race, gender, or having joined the organization through an acquisition, the guest effect may be intensified. Permission must then be addressed as a core issue in the leadership brand management effort. Ironically, sometimes when a key individual leaves an organization because of lack of fit with the team, it's often less about people clashing, and more about the individual's insufficient sense of permission. When players relegate themselves to guest status, they become the source of their own conflict with organizational fit. Once the matter of permission is rectified, other aspects of fit—most often style-related—can be addressed by analyzing the individual's persona and where it does and does not align with market needs and norms.

Imposter syndrome

Permission, so essential to creating and managing a strong brand, also poses a challenge to people who suffer from Imposter Syndrome. This is a well-documented phenomenon concerning self-doubt, and research indicates it afflicts women more often than men. Professional women who are successful, intelligent, and highly capable may spend their days distracted or consumed by feelings of not being good enough. They see themselves as imposters who will be revealed for who they 'really' are—high-level managers who are actually incapable; sales leaders who are incompetent; or newly promoted executives whose promotions were the result of dumb luck. In her book, *Play Like a Man, Win Like a Woman,* Gail Evans writes about the stunning impact of Imposter Syndrome. She describes a scenario where someone "asks you a question that you can't answer. And when that time comes, you suspect that you're an imposter. This is the horrible, sinking feeling, experienced by the intelligent and the hardworking, that success is accidental. This imposter syndrome causes us to live in constant fear that we will be discovered, that our inadequacies will be exposed."

Does this sound familiar? Could you be suffering from imposter syndrome? Even if *you* aren't, are you leading others who are held hostage by it? In order to get the very best from your team members, they have to feel confident to fully participate, not hold back, and to appropriately express different points of view. It is in your best interest as a leader and manager of talent to learn to spot Imposter Syndrome and work to diminish its negative effects. In its own way, Imposter Syndrome produces the same negative impact on the business that an illness does. It lurks in the back of your mind, constantly sapping you of your ability to concentrate, to focus your energy on what's real, and to solve problems instead of shying away from the action in anticipation of them. For organizations and individuals to succeed, they must be free of Imposter Syndrome.

The Components of Permission

Many successful people have had to learn how to locate and lock in their own state of permission, and many find they must work at it. The outcome is that they have found a way to turn off the internal radio station of self-questioning, and especially those questions about "how I should be." Understanding the three powerful components of permission (context, clarity, and a personal support system) will help you do this.

The first component of permission is *context*. This comes with your ability to step back from any given moment—especially challenging ones—and see yourself in the totality of your track record. To see yourself in the context of a career that includes a succession of wins, and no doubt some losses and mistakes. In the broader context, your track record is a catalogue of all that you have achieved in your career. This record is 'in the bank'; it can't be taken away from you and it's not up for debate. Of your track record to date, there can be no doubt, no question, no lack of certainty. Gaining clarity requires you to do some work, to catalog your career achievements, to reflect on them, and to own them. This work can be complex, and it helps to have a skilled coach facilitate it. Once you've done this work, the next step is to ensure that you share this context, especially with brand builders, sponsors, mentors, and others who can support your continued career growth. If you don't have clarity about the essential value of your brand, how can you expect others to? Using the framework of the 5 P's of Leadership Brand® and obtaining continuous feedback helps you stay on top of this.

The third component of permission is a *personal support system*. While it's true that ultimately permission comes from within, the role of mentors and brand builders at work and other members of your support system in your personal life is to provide the reinforcement that you need, particularly as you deal with challenges or even flat-out fail. Support systems can't replace our self-validation, but they can play an important role in reinforcing it.

What's the Cost of Denying Yourself Permission to be a Member?

The cost of not fully participating, of course, is that the business doesn't get the best thinking of all its talent. For individuals, the cost can be frustration at seeing others become more visible and more valuable, while their value diminishes. The value of your leadership brand is clearly a function of the strength of your own self-permission.

Permission: One Leader's View

I'd like to pass along the views of one of my colleagues, Donna Griffin, on the importance of taking your seat at the table; of believing that you deserve and indeed must be an integral part of your organization. Donna is the Managing Director, Worldwide Operations, at Chubb Group of Insurance Companies, and has a tremendous track record of supporting leadership development on the individual and programmatic levels at Chubb both in the U.S. and abroad. She knows what organizations lose when not all players are fully self-permitting, and conversely what they gain when they are self-permitting. When I interviewed her for this book, she shared these thoughts:

"Within a business environment the question is, how do we want the workforce to feel? From a human perspective, the answer is obvious—we want people to feel empowered, responsible, and connected to their work. With this said, however, business is driven by growth and profit, and so our considerations need to go beyond the softer, people concerns. Ultimately then, the 'member versus guest' theme should be viewed within the context of organizational results, and it's my strong view that members, not guests, drive bottom line success.

"Ensuring quality is vital to the success of any product line. When business associates perceive a greater connection to their jobs, they take more pride in their work, put more effort into it, and are more concerned with the final product. Members feel a greater stake in the business and with an almost 'profit-sharing' attitude they tie the success of the organization to their own personal success.

"Attracting and retaining talent drives growth and profit. People want to work in an environment built on policies of inclusion. Good talent and experienced workers are more likely to join and remain with organizations that treat the workforce as members, as opposed to guests. From a financial perspective, the costs of hiring and the loss of intellectual capital make it prudent to retain the strong talent that is brought into the company.

"Developing leaders for the future is one of my chief tasks as an executive. All companies need a continuous influx of people who understand the business from a strategic perspective. Members are more likely to become strategic thinkers and leaders *because* they are involved and engaged. Through their interactions they see where their contributions fit into the 'big picture' and they tend to act with confidence to seize opportunities and address problems.

"As leaders, it's in our control to create members, not guests. We create the policies and we control our own interactions day-to-day with our staff. Each of us as leaders owns the outcomes of our efforts and it is clearly reflected in overall business performance."

Take Your Seat at the Table

Some players are waiting for others to legitimize them by saying, "You are worthy to participate as a member along with the rest of us." If you are waiting for this kind of invitation, please be advised that you will have a long, long wait. The truth is that you've already been invited to play! That invitation was implicit when you joined the organization. When you understand that, you finally realize that the only one really holding you back—the one who is making a guest out of a member—is *you*. Strong brands are indeed managed outcomes and each of us has extraordinary control over our own.

Kim Cromwell, a management consultant and national expert on workforce productivity and diversity, provides another example. She has seen evidence of a different kind of permission issue. "People frequently focus on the way they want to appear to others, and sometimes lose sight of what it is that makes them unique. Particularly when an individual is a member of a minority group—a person of color, a lesbian or gay man, or even a woman in an organization where the majority of employees are heterosexual white males—it is easy to project what we think our brand *should* be, rather than focusing on what we want it to be."

It is interesting to note that even those with professional training in brand awareness sometimes find themselves faltering. Kim told me that early in her career when she worked in high technology firms (typically male dominated), she found herself diminishing her own contribution, something not uncommon among women. "Before offering an idea in a meeting," she said, "I would use a qualifier like 'I may not know anything about this, but…' I thought I was being humble, which I thought was a valuable trait. In retrospect, I realize that I was demonstrating a lack of faith in my own perspective." When Kim later made a career move into a new industry, she committed to change this behavior and it paid off. She discovered that when she demonstrated faith in her own ideas, her colleagues reflected her confidence. "It was as if I created a self-fulfilling prophecy," she says. "Plus, I felt I was being more honest with myself. I knew I had something of value to contribute, and it made no sense for me not to feel good about that." In other words, when she gave herself permission, she reaped benefits two ways: her colleagues and managers viewed her as a more valuable player, paving the way for her to have more significant impact, value, and better opportunities; and this response to her brand made her feel appreciated for the quality of her ideas and work, and, thus, able to be authentic and impactful in her job.

Summary

Permission is clarity that you are a member, not a guest, in your organization. It is the belief that you are just as good, if not better, than others around the table; that you have just as much, if not more, to offer than the other players on the team; and that you are fully entitled to play on the same field. What's most important is that you give yourself permission to expect access as a contributing member of a successful team, and that you hold yourself accountable for creating meaningful impact for the business as a result of this permitting mindset. Taking pride in who you are and in the value you provide, and then sharing news about your value are steps you can take to begin building the foundation of a strong brand. If you are already a permitting leader, recognize the responsibility you have to ensure others feel as included and entitled to contribute as you do.

Update your Brand Development Plan Worksheet now

Take a moment now to fill in the permission section of your Brand Management Plan Worksheet with a few statements about your right to a seat at the table. Make sure these are strong, positive statements of your worth and entitlement to an opportunity to join the team. If you suffer from Imposter Syndrome, write in the action steps you will take to overcome it so that you can begin to believe fully in your competence and the value of your ideas.

Chapter 7

Market Feedback

A fundamental part of brand management is continuous market research. When you cited strong and favorable recall of some of the strongest brands in the world as you read the introduction to this book, you were also naming businesses that have extraordinarily evolved feedback systems—processes designed to capture and address extensive and sophisticated market intelligence about the brand's performance and how it sits in the minds of its buyers.

Once you have developed a clear sense of what your differentiated value is, your work has only just begun. Your next steps involve the continuous activity of collecting feedback to determine the degree to which your intentions for your own brand—how you choose to be understood—are in fact others' reality. Feedback will tell you what your brand is in your market, and how strong it is. Feedback will also tell you when you're relying on a dated value exchange and that it's time to upgrade it to keep pace with changing customer and market needs. How do you learn the answers to all these questions? There's only one way: You have to ask.

Remember when we talked about emotional intelligence in Chapter 2? Emotional intelligence (the ability to recognize and deal with feelings and emotions and to manage them in ourselves and our relationships) is essential to obtaining good feedback about leadership brands. Emotional competencies also play a huge role in superior job performance. Leaders with great brands have emotional intelligence and possess a combination of self-acceptance, self-awareness, and self-improvement in part because they did the difficult work of asking for feedback, and then acted on it.

Your research into your brand will help you stay current with how it is performing and how it is perceived vis-à-vis the changing needs of the market. Keeping an open mind about the feedback you get will help you keep your brand current and powerful. As with all aspects of brand management, you decide what to do with what you learn; the research simply gives you knowledge about the perceptions of your brand. Your job is to know what those perceptions are and then make conscious decisions, in accordance with your values, about how to manage them.

How to Get Useful Feedback

It is difficult for service suppliers in organizations to obtain solid, useful feedback. The reasons are numerous, but most often it's because giving constructive feedback is hard. Your colleagues, co-workers, and customers when asked may shy away from giving you anything but polite compliments. They may be concerned that you'll react badly to negative feedback, or they simply may not know how to share difficult feedback. Their desire to be liked by you may prevent them from engaging in a discussion that might jeopardize the relationship.

You play a central role in creating the climate that enables others to share balanced, constructive feedback with you. If you want real power—the power of knowing the attributes and drags of your brand—you have to get feedback. Your job is to make it safe for others to provide you with what you need to know.

Constructive feedback usually addresses two areas: what is working well and what could be working better (or needs to be changed). Feedback may suggest that something should be added to your brand experience or capability, or subtracted because it doesn't enhance your brand. When we get honest feedback, we know it. Its truth makes us smile—or wince. When we hear that something worked well in a presentation that we just made, we feel good. Conversely, when we get feedback on something that we didn't do as well—feedback that stings a little—we wince.

The smile-wince factor is important in evaluating feedback. It helps you confirm that you got good information, not just a polite response. It's similar to a good workout at the gym—the process involves some pain, but the end result is your own increased fitness, strength, and confidence.

Ask the Right Questions

Just as regular exercise keeps you sharp and healthy over the long run, feedback enables you to effectively manage your brand today and over the course of your career. Without feedback, you may lose your edge or, conversely, keep a rough edge that should be smoothed out to enhance working relationships. But you'll never know unless you not only ask, but also ask in a way that elicits the full story.

In my work with professional women, particularly women of color, I am reminded repeatedly of the difficulty of getting robust, honest, direct feedback. In general, if we're reluctant to be critical of others, imagine how the situation is further complicated when race, gender, and ethnicity are part of the mix. Women of color who have successfully worked through this issue can teach everyone how to get good feedback. In general, these women succeed because they take the initiative to get feedback and do three things as part of the process:

- They prepare themselves to hear the positives and the negatives, what they can do better, and what isn't working.

- They work at being relaxed when asking for feedback to put the other person at ease.

- They choose language that keeps the conversation neutral and objective: What's one thing that's working? What's one thing I can do better next time? What can I do differently to take my performance to the next level? If my goal is to be a division executive in a couple of years, what are the most important things to focus on to get there? What skills and personal qualities do you think are necessary to be a successful leader in this organization?

Notice that the last question was not personalized. Even so, the respondent will usually answer the question by providing information specifically about the person who is asking. Remember, the most powerful feedback doesn't *presuppose* what matters to others in your market—open-ended questions are key to getting at what really matters to *them*.

Survey Instruments

All of the questions and methods above are useful in getting a sense of your marketplace's perception of you. Of course, there are other ways. Asking for informal feedback *of the moment* is one. The typical 360-degree survey is another. These surveys usually have a litany of competencies already described, and they ask you to rate a person on a scale of 1–5 on the competencies. While 360-degree feedback instruments obtain input from employees above you, beside you, and below you on a predetermined list of competencies, these competencies don't always reflect the true priorities and needs of your particular market.

To get at the true driving forces of any given marketplace, my firm has developed a customized market research instrument that helps our clients discover how their brand is performing and the degree to which their value exchange meets the *specific* needs of those in *their* marketplace. This proprietary survey instrument is beneficial because it captures what the *respondent* is paying attention to. It doesn't presuppose what's most important to a market and the individuals in it. Rather, through its unique design, it elicits extraordinarily powerful and useful information about how well (or poorly) a leader's brand is aligning with market needs. If you believe that knowledge is power, then this type of information can make you powerful indeed as it shows you what you can do to enhance your brand to have a bigger impact on your organization.

In effect it ensures that 'all the lights are on in the room' when it comes to your brand. Once you know how you exist in the minds of those in your market, you are in control—you can make intelligent, values-driven choices about what you can and must do to advance toward your goals. Imagine how useful it would have been for Larry, presented in the story at the golf course at the very beginning of this book, if he had known how his CEO perceived him. Imagine all that he had in his power to change the CEO's perception that day at the golf course, but because he didn't do his homework and didn't get the CEO's perspective, he instead sabotaged himself.

Whatever method you use, your goal is to truly hear the voice of your market, and to ensure that this intelligence informs your brand development and decision-making. Soliciting feedback takes courage, and once you start doing it, it's to your great benefit to keep doing it. Obtaining feedback is much like getting regular exercise—it's much less painful when it's integrated into your ongoing routine. Really strong brands are only strong because the brand managers constantly collect feedback in a variety of ways, from a variety of stakeholders.

How to Handle the Feedback

Strong leaders are often controversial. Their employees all have opinions of their performance and personality. These leaders are governed by a vision of how things could be better, and they bring a sense of optimism to their view of the world and the workplace. They are change agents, and, as such, they are hungry for feedback. They know they can't succeed if others don't share their vision and a desire to realize that vision. So instead of having a knee-jerk response to feedback ("This made some people really mad; I better change my plan" or "They're picking apart everything I do; they should stop whining"), they make conscious decisions about what to do or not do *as a result of feedback*. Strong leaders know that being respected, respecting others, being trusted, and having the utmost integrity are the keys to leading. They also know, from experience, that even when these factors are present, they are not guarantees of popularity. It is lonely at the top.

As you continue to evolve as a leader, you can anticipate receiving feedback that speaks to your strengths *and* to your needs for development. Your task will be to make smart decisions about which aspects of the feedback you will attend to as you work to achieve your goals. The example of Elaine presented in Chapters 2 and 3 is illustration of this. Ultimately, feedback should help you explore what is working really well, and what is standing in the way of you implementing your vision for your business and yourself.

What to Do with What You Learn

Once you've learned how your market understands you, the most important thing is to let the information settle a bit. Sit back. Reflect. Begin to look for places where your market's understanding of you aligns with your intentions. *Do not* respond immediately to all of the suggested feedback about improvements and changes. Instead, take a break to put some distance between the feedback and your immediate (and probably emotional) reaction to it. Then, return to the data and work through the following process:

■ Spend as much time as you need acknowledging the strengths of your brand. This is extremely important because these strengths are the essence of your value exchange. Women, in particular, tend to discount the messages about strengths in their feedback, rushing past them and focusing instead on their brand drags. This is a mistake, as we saw in the chapter on permission. Effective analysis of your research requires that you understand it in a balanced context, beginning with what your market values about you.

■ Once you are clear about your strengths, consider your market's sense of the drags on your brand (aspects of your brand that create friction and slow you down in reaching your ideal in your marketplace). These might include minor issues (punctuality or sloppy communication) or more significant items (inability to think strategically and innovate). Feedback on the latter might sound like this: "Get out of the weeds and start thinking and acting within a broader strategic framework"; "introduce innovation into an aspect of your operations"; "stop being passive, and step out and lead"; "encourage risk-taking by being more optimistic and less critical."

■ Get back to those who provide you with feedback, and say just one thing: Thank you. No need to edify or go into what you learned or over-disclose. Just "Thanks, it was really helpful and I appreciate your taking the time."

■ Discuss what you've learned with the right person. This might be your manager, who, ideally, is also a trusted coach; your external coach; your mentor; or any smart person with whom you can have a confidential, balanced discussion of the findings. This person should be someone who can help validate themes in the feedback and support your development and implementation of an action plan.

Summary

Brands exist only in the context of a marketplace. As you read this book, remember that you have a brand, right now, and it is affecting everything about your work: your ability to have impact, your own fulfillment, your mobility, your compensation, and much more. Feedback is the only way you know how you show up in your market; how tightly aligned your intentions are with others' realities. Gathering, analyzing and acting intelligently on your brand feedback is essential to your ability to be a competitive, viable service supplier whose strong value exchange evolves to meet changing market needs. Routinely obtaining—and appropriately acting upon—feedback about your brand is the only way to ensure that it is, and will continue to be, strong and differentiated. By combining your self-assessment of your brand with feedback from your market, you will have a solid understanding of your current state and what, if any, changes you need to make to maintain a strong brand.

Update your Brand Development Plan Worksheet now

Now you are ready to fill in the last part of your Brand Development Plan Worksheet by writing the names of colleagues, managers, subordinates, and others from whom you will solicit feedback. Jot down questions you want to ask, making sure they are in the neutral format suggested in this chapter.

Conclusion

Your brand is how you live in the hearts and minds of those in your market. It is what comes to mind for people when your name surfaces in casual discussions in the hallway to formal succession planning deliberations. It has everything to do with the way you conduct yourself, the way you communicate, the choices you make, and the opportunities you pursue throughout your career. Strong brands are intentional, deliberate, managed outcomes. They are not accidental or coincidental. If you have a strong brand, it is because you have made it so. If not, the same is true.

Strong brands begin from within. Your brand is rooted in your vision and your values—those you live by personally and those you have in your role as a leader or aspiring leader in your organization. From this core, you build your brand by tapping into your unique strengths to create differentiated value for your organization marketplace. The 5 P's—persona, product, packaging, promotion, and permission—provide you with a systematic way to identify the many important components of your unique brand and enable you to actively manage it.

Owning a strong brand requires ongoing focus, attention, and discipline. The method described in this book helps you maintain that focus and manage your brand as marketplace dynamics change. Keeping your brand fit through attention to the 5 P's requires the same rigor and discipline as keeping yourself fit through exercise and nutrition. It is an ongoing, never-ending process that takes genuine effort, especially as one approaches mid-career, a time when competing priorities, pressures, and personal changes seem to increase.

If you were filling in your Brand Development Plan Worksheet as you were reading, you are now ready to take charge of your brand. Your plan, coupled with ongoing solicitation of market feedback and your intelligent response to it, will help you bring your brand of excellence and integrity to your organization marketplace.

What work do you have to do in persona, product, packaging, promotion, and permission to make your brand powerful? Which aspects of your brand development need immediate attention? Which aspects should you preserve or grow, and which should you change? Whose support will you need to execute your plan? What impact will your unique set of strengths bring to your organization's bottom line? These are questions that you will want to ask yourself on a regular basis to keep your brand strong.

Strong brands are managed outcomes. One year from today, what do you want your brand to be? To realize that vision, what steps will you take today and *every day*? What will you do to ensure your market perceives you as you want to be perceived?

It is my hope that the ideas, tools, and methods presented in this book will enable you to become a distinctive leader—guided by your own inspiring vision, a steadfast commitment to your core values, and the pursuit of your own quest to create an extraordinary future for yourself, your team and your marketplace.

> *If one advances confidently in the direction of his dreams, and endeavors to live the life which he has imagined, he will meet with a success unexpected in common hours.*
>
> —*Henry David Thoreau*

Brand Development Plan Worksheet

Element	Brand Attributes	Brand Drags	Desired Changes	Action Required
Persona				
Product				
Packaging				
Promotion				
Permission				
Market Feedback				

Notes

Chapter 1

American Marketing Association, 311 South Wacker Drive, Suite 5800, Chicago, IL 60606.

Chapter 2

Aaker, David A. *Building Strong Brands.* New York: The Free Press, 1996.

Buckingham, Marcus, and Curt Coffman. *First Break All the Rules.* New York: Simon and Schuster, 1999.

Goleman, Daniel. *Working with Emotional Intelligence.* New York: Bantam Books, 1998.

Maccoby, Michael. "Narcissistic Leaders: The Incredible Pros, the Inevitable Cons." Harvard Business Review, January-February 2000.

Rutledge, Thom. *Embracing Fear.* San Francisco: Harper, 2002.

Chapter 3

Bennis, Warren. *Learning to Lead.* New York: Perseus, 1997.

Covey, Stephen. *The 7 Habits of Highly Effective People.* New York: Simon & Schuster, 1989.

Keirsey, David. *Please Understand Me II.* Del Mar, CA: Prometheus Nemesis Book Company, 1998.

Chapter 5

Hymowitz, Carol, *The Wall Street Journal*, Feb. 9, 2004.

Chapter 6

Evans, Gail. *Play Like a Man, Win Like a Woman.* New York: Broadway Books, 2000.

Suggested Reading

Aaker, David A. *Building Strong Brands*. New York: The Free Press, 1996.

Advancing Women in Business: Best Practices from the Corporate Leaders. Catalyst research and publications, 120 Wall Street, New York, NY 10005. www.catalystwomen.org

Bell, E., and S. Nkomo. *Our Separate Ways: Black and White Women and the Struggle for Professional Identity*. Boston: Harvard Business School Press, 2001.

Bennis, Warren. *Learning to Lead*. New York: Perseus, 1997.

Bennis, Warren. *On Becoming a Leader*. New York: Perseus, 2003.

Bristol, Claude M. *The Magic of Believing*. New York: Pocket Books, 1991.

Buckingham, Marcus, and Curt Coffman. *First, Break all the Rules: What the World's Greatest Managers Do Differently*. New York: Simon & Schuster, 1999.

Covey, Stephen. *The 7 Habits of Highly Effective People*. New York: Simon & Schuster, 1989.

D'Alessandro, David. *Career Warfare: 10 Rules for Building A Successful Personal Brand and Fighting to Keep It*. New York: McGraw-Hill, 2004.

Ellig, J., and W. Morin. *What Every Successful Woman Knows.* New York: McGraw-Hill, 2001.

Evans, Gail. *Play Like a Man, Win Like a Woman.* New York: Broadway Books, 2000.

Goleman, Daniel. *Working with Emotional Intelligence.* New York: Bantam Books, 1998.

Heskett, J., W. Earl Sasser, and L. Schlesinger. *The Service Profit Chain: How Leading Companies Link Profit and Growth to Loyalty, Satisfaction and Value.* New York: The Free Press, 1997.

Keirsey, David. *Please Understand Me II.* Del Mar, CA: Prometheus Nemesis Book Company, 1998.

Kouzes, J., and B. Posner. *The Leadership Challenge,* 3rd Ed. San Francisco: Jossey-Bass, 2003.

Markides, Constantinos. *All the Right Moves: A Guide to Crafting Breakthrough Strategy.* Boston: Harvard Business School Press, 2000.

Rutledge, Thom. *Embracing Fear.* San Francisco: Harper, 2002.

Thomas, David A., and John Gabarro. *Breaking Through: The Making of Minority Executives in Corporate America.* Boston: Harvard Business School Press, 1999.

Treacy, Michael, and Fred Wiersema. *The Discipline of Market Leaders.* Reading, MA: Addison-Wesley, 1995.

Zander, Rosamund, and Benjamin Zander. *The Art of Possibility.* New York: Penguin Putnam, 2000.

About the Author

Susan Hodgkinson is Principal of The Personal Brand Company, and is a nationally recognized expert in the field of personal and leadership brand management. She provides executive coaching, leadership development consulting, brand consulting, and presentation coaching to clients in the for-profit and not-for-profit sectors. Her expertise is built upon her success as a marketing and public relations professional working inside organizations in healthcare, financial services, and state government. She launched her company in 1994.

Ms. Hodgkinson is the creator of the proprietary The 5 P's of Leadership Brand® and Personal Brand Management methodologies, which she has applied in coaching and workshop settings with thousands of professionals throughout the U.S. to show them how to succeed by managing their professional learning, leadership development, and personal brands. Clients include professionals at all levels in organizations, including men, women, and people of color, who have significantly increased their impact, confidence, and career mobility through this work.

Hodgkinson received her MBA from the Simmons School of Management in Boston. She is a competitive triathlete, and lives with her family in Massachusetts.

To contact Susan Hodgkinson and The Personal Brand Company, visit www.ThePersonalBrandCompany.com.

Index

978-0-595-67307-0
0-595-67307-4

Printed in the United States
106829LV00003B/10/A

9 780595 673070